Disability Law Secrets

Everyday Rights You Might Not Know About

Disability Law Secrets

Everyday Rights You Might Not Know About

Jana Lomax, J.D.

Civil Rights Lawyer and Investigator

Disability Law Secrets - Everyday Rights You Might Not Know About

Copyright © 2024 by Jana Lomax, J.D.

All rights reserved.

Fb.com/janallomaxjd

All characters and events portrayed in this book are fictitious. Any similarity to real persons, living or dead, is coincidental and not intended by the author.

No part of this book may be reproduced in any form or by any means without express written permission of the author.

ISBN-13: 9798303196155

Printed in the United States of America

Legal Disclaimer: The content of this book is for informational purposes only and should not be construed as legal advice. While the book provides valuable insights into disability law, it does not establish an attorney-client relationship between the author and the reader. I am not responsible for any actions taken (or not taken) based on the information provided in the book.

Each legal situation is unique, and the information in this book may not apply to your specific circumstances. For personalized legal advice, you should consult a qualified attorney. I disclaim any liability for any outcomes resulting from the use of the information in this book. All content is provided "as is" and I make no representations about the accuracy, completeness, or timeliness of the information. Only a licensed attorney can provide tailored advice that is appropriate to your situation.

Thank you for using this book as a resource, but please remember it's not a substitute for professional legal counsel.

Table of Contents

    Disability Law Secrets - Everyday Rights You Might Not Know About x

Introduction – Empowering Yourself with Knowledge xvi

    Purpose of the Book xvi

    Who Should Read This Book xvii

    What This Book Covers xix

Chapter 1: Key Disability Rights Laws You Need to Know 1

    The Americans with Disabilities Act (ADA) 1

    Section 504 of the Rehabilitation Act 2

    Fair Housing Act (FHA) 3

    Other Relevant Laws 4

Chapter 2: Recognizing and Addressing Discrimination 10

    Types of Discrimination 10

    Recognizing Discrimination in Action 13

    How to Address Discrimination 15

Chapter 3: Your Rights in Education 17

    Understanding Your Educational Rights Under Federal Laws......................................17

    Equal Access in Education 18

    Securing Accommodations in Education 19

    Reasonable Accommodations in Higher Education...20

    Special Laws in Education for Students with Disabilities..21

    Examples of Disability Discrimination in Education 27

Chapter 4: Your Rights in Employment 31

    ADA Protections in the Workplace 31

    Requesting Accommodations 33

    Special Laws in Employment for Individuals with Disabilities..35

    Recognizing Discrimination 39

    Examples of Disability Discrimination in Employment 40

    Pregnancy Discrimination 46

Chapter 5: Access to Public Services and Spaces 51

    Public Accommodations 51

    Disability Discrimination in Public Accommodations 57

Chapter 6: Housing Rights and Fair Housing 65

    Fair Housing Act 65

    Special Laws Related to Disability in Housing 66

    Dealing with Housing Discrimination 72

    Examples of Disability Discrimination in Housing 74

Chapter 7: Healthcare Rights and Medical Advocacy 80

    Equal Access to Healthcare 80

    Special Laws in Healthcare for Individuals with Disabilities 81

    Advocating for Yourself in Healthcare Settings 86

    Resolving Healthcare Barriers 87

    Examples of Disability Discrimination in Healthcare 89

Chapter 8: Transportation Rights 95

    ADA and Transportation 95

    Private Transportation: Rights to Accommodations in Taxis, Ridesharing, and Airlines .97

    Special Laws in Public and Private Transportation Services for Individuals with Disabilities 98

    How to Address Transportation Barriers 102

    Examples of Disability Discrimination in Transportation 104

Chapter 9: Building Confidence as an Advocate 109

    Self-Advocacy Tips 109

Chapter 10: Connecting with Support Networks 114

    Advocacy Groups and Communities 114

    Building a Personal Support System 116

    Allies 117

    Tips for Building and Maintaining Support Networks 118

Chapter 11: Practical Tools for Navigating Daily Life 119

    Where to File a Disability-Related Complaint 119

    Sample Templates 124

    Checklists and Action Plans 127

    Steps to Take When Discrimination Occurs 128

    Helpful Resources 128

Appendices .... A

    Appendix A: Key Laws and Legal References for Further Reading .... A

    Appendix B: Glossary of Terms and Acronyms C

Appendix C: Online and Local Resources ....F

To all the warriors navigating the world of disability rights—you are the trailblazers, the change-makers, and the ones who refuse to settle for anything less than equality. This book is for you, to help you reclaim your power, assert your rights, and move through the world with the confidence you deserve. Your journey may not always be easy, but your strength and resilience are unstoppable. Keep pushing forward, keep fighting for your future, and remember: your voice can change the world.

"The world needs all kinds of minds."

— **Temple Grandin**, autism advocate and professor

Disability Law Secrets - Everyday Rights You Might Not Know About

Disability laws extend far beyond the workplace or healthcare systems—they're woven into daily life in ways that often go unnoticed. The world is gradually becoming more inclusive, thanks to a range of laws and regulations that safeguard the rights of individuals with disabilities. Disability laws touch nearly every aspect of daily life, ensuring inclusivity and accessibility in ways that are often surprising. From amusement parks to grocery shopping, these laws empower individuals with disabilities to fully participate and enjoy the world around them, often in surprising and creative ways.

Here are just a few examples of how disability rights extend to some unexpected areas of life. Read on for even more in-depth explorations throughout this book.

---

1. Movie Theater Accessibility

Under the Americans with Disabilities Act (ADA), movie theaters are required to provide devices that make the movie-going experience inclusive. These include closed captioning for those who are deaf or hard of hearing and audio description devices for individuals who are blind or visually impaired. With these accommodations, everyone can enjoy the latest blockbuster, ensuring that entertainment is truly accessible for all.

2. Miniature Horses as Service Animals

While dogs are the most common service animals, the ADA also recognizes miniature horses. These highly intelligent and trainable animals can assist individuals with disabilities in various ways, including guiding those with visual impairments and providing stability for individuals with mobility challenges. They're even permitted in public spaces when they meet the ADA's criteria, which include being housebroken and under the handler's control.

3. Hotel Pools and Spas

Hotels must ensure that their pools and spas are accessible to individuals with disabilities. This may include installing pool lifts or sloped entry ramps that allow wheelchair users to enter the water with ease. These accommodations ensure that everyone, regardless of their physical abilities, can relax and enjoy the water.

4. **Grocery Store Accommodations**

Grocery stores increasingly offer services that cater to individuals with disabilities. From personal shopping assistance to sensory-friendly shopping hours designed for people with autism or sensory processing disorders, these efforts make grocery shopping more inclusive. Accessible checkout lanes, motorized carts, and carry-out assistance also ensure that individuals with mobility challenges can shop comfortably and independently.

5. **Website Accessibility**

The ADA requires that websites be designed or updated to accommodate people with disabilities. Features like screen reader compatibility, alt text for images, and keyboard-only navigation help ensure that individuals with visual, motor, or cognitive impairments can access essential online services, such as shopping, banking, and education. As the digital world grows, web accessibility is increasingly vital.

6. **Air Travel Rights**

The Air Carrier Access Act (ACAA) ensures that people with disabilities can travel by air with dignity and ease. Airlines must provide assistance for boarding and deplaning, accommodate mobility devices at no extra charge, and make lavatories accessible on larger planes. These rights enable individuals with disabilities to travel more freely and enjoy the same opportunities as others.

7. **Service Animals in Training**

Service animals don't become helpers overnight—they need extensive training in public environments to prepare for their future roles. Many states recognize the importance of this process by granting service animals in training access to public spaces like restaurants, stores, and public transportation. This allows trainers to teach them vital skills that will enable independence for individuals with disabilities.

8. **Disability Plates and Parking Perks**

Obtaining a disability placard or plate often comes with benefits like waived parking fees and extended time limits at parking meters. These perks reduce the stress of finding parking and provide equitable access to parking spaces close to destinations, especially in crowded urban areas.

9. Inclusive Playgrounds and Parks

Modern playgrounds and parks are designed with accessibility in mind. Wheelchair-friendly paths, adaptive play equipment, and sensory-friendly areas ensure that children with disabilities can enjoy playtime alongside their peers. These inclusive spaces also offer opportunities for families to spend time together in welcoming environments.

10. Amusement Park Accessibility

Amusement parks are no longer off-limits for individuals with disabilities. Many parks now offer accommodations such as accessible ride vehicles, alternate experiences for guests unable to board certain attractions, and sensory-friendly spaces. In some cases, people with disabilities can even receive front-of-the-line access to minimize wait times, creating a more enjoyable experience.

11. Public Restroom Standards

Public restrooms are required to meet ADA standards, making them usable for people with various disabilities. This includes features like accessible stalls with grab bars, sinks mounted at wheelchair-accessible heights, and enough space to maneuver mobility devices. These design standards ensure that everyone can use public facilities with dignity and ease.

12. Assistive Technology at Work and School

Technology plays a critical role in accessibility. At work and school, individuals with disabilities have the right to request assistive tools like screen readers, speech-to-text software, or braille materials. These accommodations level the playing field and ensure that people with disabilities can participate fully in educational and professional environments.

13. Zoo and Aquarium Sensory-Friendly Days

Many zoos and aquariums host sensory-friendly events tailored for individuals with autism or sensory processing disorders. These events feature quieter environments, dimmed lighting, and reduced crowds, allowing attendees to enjoy exhibits without feeling overwhelmed. Quiet zones and sensory kits with noise-canceling headphones or fidget tools are often available.

14. Disability Tax Deductions

The IRS provides tax deductions for disability-related expenses. These include the cost of medical equipment, home modifications (such as installing ramps or widening doorways), and service animal care. These deductions ease the financial burden of necessary accommodations and services.

15. Emergency Evacuation Plans

Safety during emergencies is crucial for everyone, including individuals with disabilities. Employers and public spaces must have evacuation plans that address accessibility, such as providing evacuation chairs for multi-story buildings, training staff on assisting individuals with disabilities, and ensuring that emergency exits are wheelchair-accessible.

16. Work-from-Home Rights

Remote work, once considered a luxury, is now recognized as a reasonable accommodation under the ADA. For individuals with chronic illnesses, mobility challenges, or mental health conditions, the ability to work from home can make the difference between maintaining employment and facing unnecessary barriers.

17. Inclusive Fitness Centers

Fitness centers are increasingly providing accessible equipment, such as hand cycles, adjustable weight machines, and treadmills with grab bars. Many gyms also offer classes and personal training tailored to individuals with disabilities, making physical fitness accessible to all.

18. Subtitles and Audio for Streaming Platforms

Streaming platforms like Netflix and Hulu have embraced accessibility by offering customizable subtitles and audio descriptions. These features enable people with hearing or visual impairments to enjoy movies, TV shows, and documentaries alongside their friends and families.

19. Sensory-Friendly Movie Screenings

Select movie theaters host sensory-friendly screenings, where the sound is lowered, the lights are dimmed but not fully darkened, and audience members are free to move around as needed. These screenings are particularly beneficial for people with autism, sensory processing disorders, or anxiety, creating a more inclusive cinema experience.

20. Public Transit Accessibility

The ADA mandates that public transportation systems accommodate people with disabilities. This includes features like wheelchair lifts on buses, designated priority seating, and clear audio or visual announcements for upcoming stops. These measures ensure that everyone can navigate their community independently.

21. Service Animals in Hospitals

Service animals are generally allowed in hospitals to accompany their handlers, as long as their presence doesn't compromise safety. For example, they may not be allowed in sterile environments like operating rooms, but they can provide vital assistance in patient rooms or during medical appointments.

22. Accessible National Parks

The National Park Service offers accessibility options that make exploring nature more inclusive. From wheelchair-friendly trails and adaptive camping gear to sign language interpreters for ranger-led programs, these accommodations allow individuals with disabilities to experience the beauty of America's national parks.

This list highlights just a few examples of how disability rights laws touch everyday life in unexpected ways. Throughout this book, you'll discover even more instances of how these regulations are transforming accessibility and inclusion for everyone.

Introduction – Empowering Yourself with Knowledge

Living with a disability —whether it's physical, neurological, mental, or sensory— in a world that wasn't designed with you in mind can often feel isolating, frustrating, and overwhelming. But it doesn't have to be that way. Understanding your rights isn't just about being informed—it's about gaining the power to stand up for yourself, make informed choices, and take control of your daily life. This book is designed to give you the knowledge, tools, and confidence to do just that.

Purpose of the Book

Disability Secrets - Everyday Rights You Might Not Know About is here to make sure you understand the laws that protect your rights and empower you to use them effectively. The laws surrounding disability rights can be complicated, and it's easy to feel lost in a sea of legal jargon. But the truth is, those laws exist for you—to ensure you can participate fully in society and receive equal treatment in your home, work, and community. This book breaks it down, offering clear and practical information about how you can use your rights to make life a little easier, safer, and more fulfilling.

You'll learn how to navigate complex systems—from the workplace to healthcare—understanding the protections that already exist for you, and how to assert those rights. By the end of this book, you'll not only know what your rights are, but how to advocate for them in a way that feels natural, powerful, and effective.

Why is understanding your disability rights so important? Because it's not just about knowing the rules—it's about knowing how to use them. Too often, people with disabilities are faced with barriers they don't know how to challenge, whether it's a lack of access to public services, discrimination at work, or not receiving the accommodations they need in healthcare. The good news is, these challenges don't have to be faced alone. This book is your roadmap, showing you where to turn when you face discrimination, unfair treatment, or outright ignorance about disability rights.

Throughout the chapters, you'll find accessible, no-nonsense explanations of the laws that protect you, whether you're navigating your rights in education, healthcare, employment, or public spaces. With each section, you'll gain insight into the practical steps you can take to ensure that your rights are respected and upheld—whether you're talking to your boss, applying for a job, or simply trying to navigate a building that's not as accessible as it should be.

By the end of this book, you'll have a deeper understanding of how the law supports you, but more importantly, how you can use that law to advocate for your needs. Knowing your rights is more than just a tool—it's the key to living life on your own terms.

Who Should Read This Book

This book is for anyone living with a disability—whether physical, neurological, mental, or sensory—who has ever felt marginalized or overlooked. Whether you're dealing with a visible disability like mobility impairments or something less visible like a neurological condition, mental health challenge, or learning disability, this guide will equip you with the knowledge to stand up for yourself and navigate a world that wasn't built with you in mind.

It's also for the caregivers, family members, and loved ones of individuals with disabilities who want to better understand the rights of those they care for. If you're supporting someone who's facing discrimination, barriers to accessibility, or challenges in getting the accommodations they need, this book will give you the tools to advocate more effectively and help create a more inclusive environment for them.

This book is for anyone who has faced discrimination, exclusion, or inequality because of their disability. If you've experienced challenges accessing education, work, or healthcare, this guide will help you understand how to advocate for the accommodations and support you're entitled to. It's also for anyone who feels uncertain about how to handle the barriers that come with living in a world that wasn't designed with disability in mind.

This book is for anyone who has ever felt overwhelmed or unsure about where to start when it comes to understanding your rights, whether it's how to request an accommodation at work, what to do when faced with discrimination, or how to navigate housing laws. It will walk you through practical steps, real-life scenarios, and clear information on the laws that protect you, giving you the tools to approach everyday challenges with a sense of power and confidence.

This book is for anyone who refuses to settle for less, who believes that they deserve to be treated with dignity, fairness, and respect. It's for anyone ready to learn how to speak up, challenge barriers, and navigate a world that's often unaccommodating. If you're ready to take control of your life, your access, and your opportunities, then this book is for you.

What This Book Covers

This book is thoughtfully organized into sections that address the most critical aspects of life where disability rights are often challenged. Each chapter equips you with the knowledge and tools needed to navigate everyday situations with confidence and stand up to discrimination. Here's what you can expect:

- **Chapter 1: Key Disability Rights Laws**
  Learn the foundational legal protections for individuals with disabilities and how they apply to various areas of life.

- **Chapter 2: Recognizing and Addressing Discrimination**
  Identify subtle and overt forms of discrimination and discover practical strategies to address them effectively.

- **Chapter 3: Disability Rights in Education**
  Understand your rights to equal access and accommodations at every level of education, from primary school to higher education.

- **Chapter 4: Disability Rights in Employment**
  Explore workplace protections, reasonable accommodations, and how to handle discrimination in the job market.

- **Chapter 5: Disability Rights in Public Services and Spaces**
  Gain insight into accessibility requirements for public services, businesses, and community spaces.

- **Chapter 6: Disability Rights in Housing**
  Learn how to secure and maintain housing without fear of discrimination and advocate for necessary accommodations.

- **Chapter 7: Disability Rights in Healthcare**

Navigate the healthcare system with confidence, ensuring equitable access to medical care and services.

- **Chapter 8: Disability Rights in Transportation**
  Discover your rights in public and private transportation, including accommodations and services designed for accessibility.

- **Chapter 9: Building Confidence as an Advocate**
  Develop the skills and mindset needed to advocate for yourself and others, creating lasting change.

- **Chapter 10: Connecting with Support Networks**
  Find and engage with communities, organizations, and resources that empower individuals with disabilities.

- **Chapter 11: Practical Tools for Navigating Daily Life**
  Access tips, checklists, and resources to handle common challenges and enhance your independence. Where to file complaints.

By the end of this book, you'll not only have a thorough understanding of the legal protections available to you but also the confidence to assert your rights, advocate for your needs, and take charge of your future. Together, we'll break down systemic barriers and create a more inclusive world for us all—one step at a time.

Chapter 1: Key Disability Rights Laws You Need to Know

Living with a disability—or caring for a loved one with a disability—can feel like you're constantly navigating a world that wasn't built with you in mind. But understanding your rights isn't just about knowing the law—it's about gaining the power to stand up for yourself and ensure that you have the same opportunities and access as anyone else. In this chapter, we'll dive into the key laws that protect people with disabilities, equipping you with the knowledge to assert your rights confidently in various aspects of life.

The Americans with Disabilities Act (ADA)

What it is

The Americans with Disabilities Act (ADA) is the cornerstone of disability rights in the United States. Passed in 1990, the ADA prohibits discrimination against individuals with disabilities in all areas of public life, including employment, education, transportation, and access to public buildings and services. The ADA is comprehensive and applies to many aspects of daily life, ensuring that people with disabilities are treated fairly and given the same opportunities as those without disabilities.

Who it protects

The ADA covers individuals with physical or mental impairments that significantly limit one or more major life activities. These activities might include things like walking, hearing, seeing, speaking, or even tasks like learning or working. The ADA protects anyone who has a documented disability or who has a history of such a disability. The law applies to people with temporary, permanent, visible, and invisible disabilities alike.

Key Provisions

- **Employment (Title I):**
- Under Title I of the ADA, employers with 15 or more employees are prohibited from discriminating against qualified individuals with disabilities in hiring, firing, promotions, and other terms of employment. Employers must also provide reasonable accommodations to enable employees with disabilities to perform the

essential functions of their job. This might include modifying work schedules, altering the physical work environment, or providing special equipment.

- **Public Services and Transportation (Title II):**

    Title II of the ADA ensures that state and local government services, programs, and activities are accessible to people with disabilities. This includes access to public transportation, such as buses and trains, and requires that government buildings, parks, and services be accessible. Public transportation must also accommodate people with mobility impairments by providing accessible buses, elevators, and ramps.

- **Public Accommodations (Title III):**

    This provision ensures that businesses and nonprofit organizations open to the public cannot discriminate against people with disabilities. Public accommodations include places like hotels, restaurants, movie theaters, and stores. Businesses are required to remove physical barriers to access, such as stairs, and provide accommodations such as ramps, accessible bathrooms, and services like sign language interpreters or captioning for people with hearing impairments.

- **Telecommunications (Title IV):**

    The ADA also addresses communication barriers for people with disabilities. Title IV ensures that telephone companies provide relay services, which enable individuals who are deaf or hard of hearing to communicate over the phone through text or a third-party relay operator. This section also mandates that closed captioning be available for television programming.

Section 504 of the Rehabilitation Act

What it is

Section 504 of the Rehabilitation Act of 1973 was one of the first laws to prohibit discrimination against individuals with disabilities. It applies to any program or activity that receives federal funding, including public schools, colleges, universities, healthcare providers, and housing programs. Section 504 requires that these organizations provide equal access and opportunities for people with disabilities.

Scope and Impact

While Section 504 is similar to the ADA, it specifically targets programs that receive federal funding. It's often considered a precursor to the ADA, and its protections complement those provided under the ADA. For example, a hospital or educational institution that receives federal funding is prohibited from discriminating against people with disabilities. This law also ensures that individuals with disabilities are provided with reasonable accommodations, such as accessible facilities or support services, so they can fully participate in programs and services.

In many ways, Section 504 laid the groundwork for the broader protections that the ADA would later provide, making it a vital piece of the disability rights framework.

Fair Housing Act (FHA)

Housing Rights

The Fair Housing Act (FHA), passed in 1968, is a federal law that prohibits discrimination in housing on the basis of race, color, national origin, religion, sex, familial status, and disability. The FHA ensures that individuals with disabilities can rent, purchase, or finance housing without facing discrimination. It also ensures that landlords and property managers make reasonable accommodations for people with disabilities, such as allowing service animals or modifying the physical environment.

Accessibility in Housing

The FHA mandates that housing units must be accessible to people with disabilities, whether they are renting or purchasing a home. If a person with a disability needs to make changes to the physical structure of their home, such as adding a ramp, widening doorways, or installing grab bars in the bathroom, they have the right to request modifications. In some cases, the landlord may be required to pay for these changes, depending on the circumstances.

Additionally, individuals with disabilities can request accommodations that enable them to fully access and enjoy their homes, such as a waiver of a "no pets" policy to allow a service animal. The law requires that landlords make these accommodations, unless doing so would impose an undue hardship on the landlord.

Other Relevant Laws

- **Individuals with Disabilities Education Act (IDEA):**

    The IDEA is a critical law for students with disabilities. It ensures that children with disabilities receive a free and appropriate public education (FAPE). Schools are required to create Individualized Education Programs (IEPs) tailored to meet the needs of students with disabilities, ensuring they receive the support and accommodations they need to succeed in school. This includes specialized services such as speech therapy, physical therapy, and educational aides.

- **Air Carrier Access Act (ACAA):**

    For individuals with disabilities who travel, the ACAA ensures that airlines provide accommodations to ensure accessibility. This includes providing wheelchair assistance, priority seating for individuals with mobility issues, and allowing service animals to travel with their owners. Airlines are also required to provide accessible restrooms and ensure that communication, such as announcements or safety instructions, is accessible to all passengers.

- **State-Specific Laws:**

    While federal laws provide strong protections for individuals with disabilities, many states have additional disability rights laws that offer further protections or provide more specific rights based on local needs. For example, some states have laws requiring businesses to offer additional accommodations for people with disabilities, such as providing sign language interpreters or modifying public transportation systems. It's important to familiarize yourself with the disability rights laws in your state, as these may provide additional layers of protection beyond the federal standards.

Understanding Social Security Disability Benefits

Social Security Disability benefits (SSD) provide vital financial support for individuals unable to work due to qualifying disabilities. While the process of obtaining these benefits can seem daunting, being informed about your rights and the application process is key. SSD programs cover a wide range of disabilities, including sensory processing disorders, sensory impairments, neurological conditions, and more, ensuring support for those facing physical, mental, or developmental challenges.

Types of Social Security Disability Benefits

1. **Social Security Disability Insurance (SSDI):**
   - Designed for individuals with a strong work history who have paid into Social Security.
   - Benefits are based on your earnings record and the work credits you've accumulated.

2. **Supplemental Security Income (SSI):**
   - A needs-based program for individuals with disabilities who have limited income and resources.
   - Eligibility does not require a work history and often includes automatic qualification for Medicaid.

Who Qualifies for Benefits?

To qualify, you must meet the Social Security Administration's (SSA) definition of disability:

- A medically determinable physical, sensory, neurological, or mental impairment.
- A condition expected to last at least 12 months or result in death.
- Inability to perform "substantial gainful activity" (SGA), meaning you cannot work and earn above a certain income threshold.

Neurological, Sensory Impairments, and Sensory Processing Disorders

The SSA recognizes various conditions as qualifying disabilities, including:

- **Neurological Disorders:** Epilepsy, multiple sclerosis (MS), Parkinson's disease, traumatic brain injury (TBI), ALS, and others.

- **Sensory Impairments:** Blindness, low vision, hearing loss, and other sensory impairments that significantly limit daily activities.

- **Sensory Processing Disorders:** Conditions that affect how the brain processes sensory information, often impacting coordination, focus, and the ability to navigate environments. These may be linked to autism spectrum disorder (ASD), PTSD, or other developmental or mental health conditions.

Steps to Apply for Disability Benefits

1. **Prepare Your Documentation:**
   Gather essential records, including:
   - Medical diagnoses, test results, and doctor's notes detailing your condition.
   - Proof of how your disability limits daily activities and work ability.
   - Employment and earnings history (for SSDI).
   - Proof of income and assets (for SSI).

2. **Submit Your Application:**
   - Applications can be filed online, by phone, or in person at a Social Security office.
   - Provide as much detail as possible to reduce delays or denials.

3. **Wait for a Decision:**
   - The review process can take several months. The SSA may request additional medical evaluations or clarification.

- If denied, appeals are often successful and worth pursuing.

Appealing a Denied Claim

If your application is denied, don't give up—many claims are approved during the appeals process. Steps include:

1. **Reconsideration:** Submit new evidence or clarify misunderstandings within 60 days of receiving the denial letter.

2. **Hearing Before an Administrative Law Judge (ALJ):** Present your case and supporting documentation in person or virtually.

3. **Appeals Council Review:** If the ALJ denies your claim, request a review by the SSA Appeals Council.

4. **Federal Court:** As a final step, you may file a lawsuit in federal court if other appeals are unsuccessful.

Benefits Beyond Financial Support

1. **Healthcare Coverage:**
   - **Medicare:** Automatically available to SSDI recipients after 24 months of benefits.
   - **Medicaid:** Often granted to SSI recipients immediately upon approval.

2. **Dependent Benefits:**
   - Your spouse and children may qualify for benefits if you're approved for SSDI.

3. **Work Incentives:**
   - Programs like Ticket to Work allow you to test employment while maintaining benefits during a trial period.

Common Challenges and How to Overcome Them

1. **Insufficient Medical Evidence:**
   - Request detailed records from healthcare providers, highlighting how your condition limits your abilities.

2. **Missed Deadlines:**
   - Stay organized and submit paperwork on time. Missing deadlines can derail your claim.

3. **Complex Applications:**
   - Seek support from disability advocates or legal professionals to navigate the process.

Your Rights as an Applicant

- **Accessibility and Accommodations:** The SSA must provide materials in accessible formats and make accommodations for individuals with sensory impairments, sensory processing disorders, or other disabilities during the application process.

- **Protection from Discrimination:** Applicants cannot be denied benefits or treated unfairly based on race, gender, age, or other protected characteristics.

- **Legal Representation:** You have the right to hire an attorney or advocate to help with your application or appeals.

Empowerment Through Knowledge

Social Security Disability benefits exist to provide stability and dignity to individuals facing significant challenges. Whether your disability is sensory, neurological, physical, or mental, you have the right to access these programs. Understanding the process and your eligibility will empower you to overcome barriers, advocate for yourself, and secure the support you deserve.

With the right knowledge and resources, you can navigate the system and take charge of your future.

Summary

Laws protecting individuals with disabilities are the cornerstone of equal access to opportunities and essential services, including employment, education, housing, public spaces, and financial support like Social Security Disability benefits. Landmark legislation such as the ADA, Section 504, and the Fair Housing Act, along with Social Security programs like SSDI and SSI, empower you to advocate for your needs, request necessary accommodations, and access the resources that enable full participation in society. Understanding these rights and benefits is critical to navigating a world often not designed with disabilities in mind. Armed with the right knowledge and tools, you can break down barriers, demand fairness, and confidently assert your place in an inclusive and equitable world.

Chapter 2: Recognizing and Addressing Discrimination

Discrimination against individuals with disabilities isn't just about overt acts of exclusion; it can manifest in many forms—ranging from the obvious to the subtle, and from individual actions to structural barriers built into society. Discrimination not only hurts the people affected but also perpetuates an environment of exclusion and injustice. Understanding the many faces of discrimination is essential for anyone with a disability, or those who care for someone with a disability, so that they can take action when necessary and protect their rights. This chapter will explore different types of discrimination, how to recognize them in various aspects of life, and provide guidance on how to address it.

Types of Discrimination

Direct Discrimination

Direct discrimination is the most easily identifiable type of discrimination. It happens when a person is treated less favorably than others because of their disability. This could occur in many contexts: for instance, a job applicant with a disability may be passed over for employment, or a person with a disability may be denied entry to a public event or venue. This form of discrimination is blatant and intentional, leaving no ambiguity about its discriminatory nature. It's crucial to recognize it because it directly impacts your ability to access jobs, services, and equal opportunities.

Examples of direct discrimination include:

- **Employment:** A person with a disability being denied a job because the employer doesn't want to accommodate their needs, even though they're qualified.

- **Public Services:** A disabled person being refused service at a restaurant because the establishment lacks accessible seating or bathroom facilities.

- **Housing:** A landlord refusing to rent to a person because of their disability or because they need modifications to the property, like a wheelchair ramp.

Indirect Discrimination

Indirect discrimination occurs when a seemingly neutral policy or practice has a disproportionate or negative impact on people with disabilities. These policies might not appear discriminatory at first glance, but when examined closely, they reveal that they disproportionately affect people with disabilities because they don't take their needs into account.

For example, an employer might require all employees to work 9 a.m. to 5 p.m. without considering that some employees with disabilities, such as those with chronic illnesses, may need flexible working hours. While this policy isn't intentionally aimed at discriminating, it creates barriers for people with certain disabilities.

Examples of indirect discrimination include:

- **Workplace:** A company policy that requires all employees to attend in-person meetings but doesn't provide virtual options, making it difficult for employees with mobility impairments to participate.
- **Public Services:** A public transportation system with timetables and services that are not accessible for individuals with physical or sensory disabilities, such as buses that don't accommodate wheelchairs or stations without Braille signage.

Systemic Discrimination

Systemic discrimination refers to the broader, structural inequalities that are embedded in societal systems and institutions, making it difficult for people with disabilities to fully participate. It's harder to pinpoint than direct or indirect discrimination because it's deeply embedded in policies, practices, and social norms. However, its effects can be far-reaching and profoundly impact people's daily lives.

Systemic discrimination is often rooted in the legal, educational, healthcare, and employment systems, where individuals with disabilities may face significant barriers to equitable access. It may be built into the very way that systems operate, often without consideration of how those systems might impact individuals with disabilities.

Examples of systemic discrimination include:

- **Education System:** Schools that don't provide adequate special education programs or accessible materials for students with disabilities, leaving them at a disadvantage.

- **Healthcare System:** Medical facilities and health insurance plans that don't provide accessible accommodations, such as lack of accessible diagnostic equipment or failure to provide necessary accommodations for communication needs (e.g., sign language interpreters).

- **Employment System:** A lack of incentives for businesses to hire individuals with disabilities, or inaccessible hiring processes and workplace environments that limit the employment opportunities available to them.

Subtle Discrimination

Subtle discrimination can be the hardest to recognize, but it can be just as damaging as more overt forms of exclusion. It includes everyday actions, comments, or societal attitudes that reinforce negative stereotypes about people with disabilities. These can come in the form of patronizing remarks, pity, assumptions about what people can and cannot do, or invisible barriers that deny the autonomy and dignity of people with disabilities. Although subtle, these acts of discrimination create a culture of marginalization that adds to the challenges people with disabilities already face.

Examples of subtle discrimination include:

- **Workplace:** A manager telling an employee with a disability, "You're doing really well for someone like you," which may sound like a compliment, but it subtly reinforces the notion that a person with a disability is expected to perform below the standard.

- **Healthcare:** A doctor dismissing a patient's concerns by assuming their disability is the cause of all their health issues, rather than taking their symptoms seriously and conducting proper tests.

- **Public Spaces:** A person offering unsolicited help to someone with a disability, assuming they need assistance without asking. While this may be intended to be helpful, it reinforces the idea that people with disabilities can't manage on their own and need constant assistance.

Recognizing Discrimination in Action

Discrimination can manifest in many different contexts of life. In each of these environments, knowing how to spot discrimination when it happens is key to addressing it effectively.

Workplace

Discrimination in the workplace is one of the most common and damaging forms of discrimination. It can take many shapes, including:

- **Unequal Treatment:** If you're qualified for a job but passed over because of your disability, or if you're excluded from a promotion or opportunity because of your disability-related needs.

- **Failure to Provide Accommodations:** When an employer refuses to make reasonable adjustments, such as flexible working hours, providing assistive technologies, or modifying the workspace to meet your needs.

- **Biased Reviews:** If you are judged unfairly due to assumptions about your disability, rather than your actual work performance. This may include being given a poor performance review because of misconceptions about your ability to handle certain tasks.

Healthcare

Healthcare discrimination can be both physically and emotionally harmful. Examples of discrimination in healthcare settings include:

- **Refusal of Treatment:** Healthcare providers may refuse to treat you because of your disability, or they may provide inferior treatment compared to others.

- **Inadequate Care:** When doctors or nurses fail to provide appropriate accommodations, such as not offering alternative communication methods for patients with hearing impairments, or not adjusting medical equipment for those with physical disabilities.

- **Denial of Services:** A person with a disability may be denied necessary services, such as rehabilitation, psychological counseling, or pain management, simply because of their disability.

Housing

Access to safe and adequate housing is a fundamental right. Discrimination in housing can prevent individuals with disabilities from finding a suitable home. Some examples of housing discrimination include:

- **Exclusion:** A landlord refuses to rent to someone because of their disability or because they need accommodations, such as a modified bathroom or ramp access.

- **Failure to Provide Modifications:** A landlord refusing to allow modifications to a property, such as widening doorways or installing grab bars in the bathroom, which are necessary for individuals with disabilities to live safely.

- **Unequal Access:** Denying disabled individuals the same quality of housing services, such as not providing accessible parking or not ensuring elevators are operational for residents with mobility impairments.

Public Accommodations

Public accommodations are places and services that are open to the public, like restaurants, stores, and entertainment venues. Discrimination here includes:

- **Denying Access:** A person with a disability may be refused entry to a public place because of physical barriers, such as a lack of ramps, accessible seating, or other necessary modifications.

- **Failure to Provide Reasonable Adjustments:** This could include not providing accessible restroom facilities, failing to accommodate service animals, or not providing sign language interpreters or other forms of communication assistance.

How to Address Discrimination

If you experience discrimination, the first step is recognizing it. Once you're aware of the discrimination, it's important to take action. Here's how to handle these situations effectively:

Immediate Actions

- **Document the Incident:** The first step in addressing discrimination is to document what happened. Write down as much detail as you can about the incident: when, where, who was involved, and any witnesses. Take photos, screenshots, or keep records of emails, messages, or letters related to the discrimination.

- **Communicate the Issue:** If you feel comfortable, bring the issue up directly with the person or organization responsible. Whether it's a supervisor, a healthcare provider, or a landlord, calmly explaining your experience can sometimes resolve the issue quickly. Be clear about what happened and request the changes or accommodations that would address your concerns.

Formal Complaints

- **Internal Complaints:** If the situation isn't resolved through direct communication, consider filing a formal complaint. Many workplaces, educational institutions, and service providers have established complaint processes for addressing discrimination. These complaints are typically reviewed by human resources, legal teams, or compliance officers.

- **Government Agencies:** For more serious or widespread discrimination, you can file complaints with government agencies such as the Equal Employment Opportunity Commission (EEOC) for workplace discrimination, the U.S. Department of Housing and Urban Development (HUD) for housing discrimination, or the Department of Justice for civil rights violations.

- **Legal Action:** If the issue persists or is particularly egregious, you may need to seek legal recourse. Consult with a disability rights attorney who can help you navigate the legal process and advocate for your rights in court.

Summary

Discrimination takes many forms, from blatant exclusion to systemic barriers, and can occur in a variety of settings such as the workplace, healthcare, housing, and public accommodations. By understanding the different types of discrimination and knowing how to recognize it in action, you can better protect yourself and take steps to fight back. Whether through immediate action, filing complaints, or seeking legal assistance, you have the tools to address discrimination when it happens. Standing up for your rights isn't just about protecting yourself—it's about advocating for a world that is more inclusive and accessible to everyone, regardless of ability.

Chapter 3: Your Rights in Education

Education is a gateway to opportunity, growth, and empowerment. However, for individuals with disabilities, systemic barriers, misconceptions, and outright discrimination can make accessing a fair education a constant battle. This chapter provides a comprehensive guide to understanding your educational rights, securing the necessary accommodations, and advocating for equitable treatment in learning environments.

Understanding Your Educational Rights Under Federal Laws

Federal laws safeguard the rights of individuals with disabilities in educational settings. Understanding these laws is essential for holding institutions accountable and protecting your right to an equitable education.

The Americans with Disabilities Act (ADA):

The ADA mandates that schools—both public and private (excluding most religious institutions)—must provide equal access to education. Under Title II (public entities) and Title III (private entities), the law requires reasonable accommodations to ensure students with disabilities can fully participate in educational programs.

Section 504 of the Rehabilitation Act of 1973:

Section 504 prohibits discrimination against individuals with disabilities in programs receiving federal funding. This law applies to most public schools and many colleges and universities, requiring that they provide accommodations such as accessible classrooms, assistive technology, and modified policies to remove barriers to education.

The Individuals with Disabilities Education Act (IDEA):

IDEA focuses on ensuring that students with disabilities receive free and appropriate public education (FAPE) tailored to their individual needs. This law applies to children ages 3–21 and emphasizes early intervention, special education services, and the development of Individualized Education Programs (IEPs).

The Family Educational Rights and Privacy Act (FERPA):

FERPA protects the privacy of student education records and allows parents or eligible students (those over 18) to review and request corrections to their educational records. This can be particularly helpful in disputes over accommodations or services.

State-Specific Laws and Policies:

Many states have additional protections that go beyond federal requirements, offering more robust services or pathways for resolving disputes. Research your state's Department of Education website to familiarize yourself with these laws.

Equal Access in Education

Education should be accessible to everyone, regardless of ability. Yet, many students encounter obstacles that make participation challenging. Equal access requires schools to remove these barriers and foster an inclusive environment.

Physical Accessibility

Under the ADA and Section 504, educational institutions must ensure that facilities are physically accessible. This includes providing:

- Ramps and elevators to bypass stairs.
- Accessible restrooms and drinking fountains.
- Adjustable desks or tables for wheelchair users.
- Reserved seating arrangements that prioritize access and comfort.

If your school's facilities are inaccessible, file a written complaint with the administration. If no action is taken, escalate the issue to the Office for Civil Rights (OCR).

Digital and Technological Accessibility

In today's digital age, access to online resources and educational technology is critical. Schools must provide accessible digital materials, including:

- Screen-reader-friendly websites.
- Closed captions or transcripts for videos.

- Accessible e-books or PDF files.

If online resources are not accessible, report the issue to the school and request alternative formats.

Inclusive Teaching and Curriculum

Schools are required to ensure that students with disabilities can participate in classroom activities, group projects, and extracurricular programs. This may involve modifying teaching methods, adapting materials, or providing additional support.

Securing Accommodations in Education

Accommodations remove barriers and allow students with disabilities to succeed alongside their peers. Federal laws provide multiple pathways for obtaining these accommodations.

Individualized Education Program (IEP)

An IEP is a legally binding document that outlines specific goals, services, and accommodations tailored to a student's needs. It is available to children with disabilities covered under IDEA.

Steps to Secure an IEP:

1. **Request an Evaluation:**

   Submit a written request to the school, asking for a comprehensive assessment of the student's needs. This may include academic, physical, or psychological evaluations.

2. **Attend the IEP Meeting:**

   Meet with school staff, teachers, and specialists to discuss the results and create a plan. Bring documentation from medical providers or therapists to support your case.

3. **Review and Revise:**

Ensure the IEP specifies accommodations (e.g., speech therapy, modified testing, or one-on-one aides) and measurable goals. Review the plan annually to address changing needs.

504 Plan

A 504 Plan provides accommodations for students who do not qualify for an IEP but still require adjustments to access education.

Examples of 504 Plan Accommodations:

- Extra time on tests or assignments.
- Preferential seating.
- Assistive technology, such as speech-to-text software.
- Modified class schedules or reduced workloads.

Steps to Request a 504 Plan:

- Write to the school's 504 coordinator or principal to initiate the process.
- Provide documentation of the disability and explain how it impacts learning.
- Collaborate with school staff to draft the plan.

Reasonable Accommodations in Higher Education

Colleges and universities must provide reasonable accommodations under the ADA and Section 504. Unlike K-12 education, students must self-advocate to access these services.

How to Secure Accommodations in College:

1. **Register with Disability Services:**

   Submit documentation of your disability and request specific accommodations.

2. **Communicate with Professors:**

   Once accommodations are approved, discuss implementation with your professors.

3. **Seek Campus Support:**

Utilize tutoring centers, mental health services, or academic advisors for additional resources.

Special Laws in Education for Students with Disabilities

There are many disability-related special circumstances in education, particularly under laws like the **Individuals with Disabilities Education Act (IDEA)**, **Section 504 of the Rehabilitation Act**, and the **Americans with Disabilities Act (ADA)**. These laws ensure that students with disabilities have equal access to education, accommodations, and support services to participate fully in academic and extracurricular activities. Here are the key disability-related special circumstances in education:

1. Individualized Education Program (IEP) under IDEA

Students with qualifying disabilities are entitled to an IEP, a tailored plan designed to meet their unique educational needs.

- Includes accommodations, modifications, and goals.
- Offers specialized instruction and services (e.g., speech therapy, occupational therapy).
- IEP meetings involve parents, teachers, and specialists to determine the best course of action.

2. 504 Plans under Section 504 of the Rehabilitation Act

Students with disabilities who do not qualify for an IEP may still receive accommodations through a 504 Plan.

- Focuses on removing barriers to education (e.g., extended test time, modified seating).
- Ensures access to school programs and facilities.

3. Reasonable Accommodations in Classroom Settings

Schools must provide reasonable accommodations to students with disabilities, such as:

- Assistive technology (e.g., speech-to-text software, screen readers).
- Modified testing conditions (e.g., quiet rooms, extra time).
- Access to note-takers or interpreters.

4. Access to Extracurricular Activities

Students with disabilities must be given equal opportunities to participate in extracurricular activities, including sports, clubs, and school events.

- Schools may need to adapt activities or provide aids, such as sign language interpreters or accessible transportation.

5. Physical Accessibility

Schools must ensure their facilities are accessible to students with disabilities. Examples include:

- Wheelchair ramps, elevators, and accessible bathrooms.
- Desks and seating arrangements suitable for students with mobility issues.

6. Behavioral Interventions for Disabilities

Students with behavioral or emotional disabilities must receive appropriate support to address challenges in the classroom, such as:

- Functional Behavioral Assessments (FBAs).
- Behavior Intervention Plans (BIPs).
- Positive reinforcement and de-escalation strategies.

7. Transition Services for Post-School Life

For students with disabilities aged 16 and older, IDEA mandates transition services to prepare them for adulthood, which may include:

- Career counseling and job training.
- Assistance with college applications or vocational programs.

- Independent living skills training.

8. Access to Higher Education

Colleges and universities are required to provide accommodations for students with disabilities, such as:

- Accessible dormitories and facilities.
- Disability resource centers for academic and personal support.
- Alternative testing formats or lecture recordings.

9. Assistive Technology

Schools must provide assistive devices or technology to help students with disabilities succeed academically, such as:

- Audiobooks for students with visual impairments.
- Augmentative communication devices for students with speech disabilities.

10. Non-Discrimination in Admissions

Students with disabilities cannot be denied admission to schools, programs, or courses based solely on their disability.

11. Service Animals in Schools

Students with disabilities may bring service animals to school, even if the school has a no-pet policy. This applies to animals trained to assist with physical, sensory, or emotional needs.

12. Accommodations for Standardized Testing

Students with disabilities are entitled to accommodations for state and national standardized tests, such as:

- Extra time or breaks.
- Alternative formats (e.g., Braille, large print).
- Testing in a distraction-free environment.

13. Protection from Harassment and Bullying

Schools must protect students with disabilities from harassment or bullying related to their disability.

- Immediate investigation of complaints is required.
- Anti-bullying policies must address disability-related harassment.

14. Homebound or Hospital-Based Instruction

Students with disabilities who are unable to attend school due to medical conditions may be eligible for homebound or hospital-based instruction.

- Schools must provide teachers or tutors to ensure continued education.

15. Support During Medical Emergencies

Schools must have plans in place to assist students with medical needs, such as:

- Access to medication during the school day (e.g., insulin, inhalers).
- Staff trained in emergency care for specific disabilities (e.g., seizure disorders).

16. Equal Access to Early Childhood Education

Preschools and early childhood programs that receive federal funding must accommodate children with disabilities, ensuring they have access to:

- Inclusive classrooms.
- Early intervention services for developmental delays.

17. Language and Communication Access

Students with communication disabilities must have access to interpreters, alternative communication methods, or specialized instruction to meet their language needs.

18. Disability-Related Absences

Students with chronic illnesses or conditions may require flexibility in attendance policies.

- Schools must excuse absences related to the disability and provide opportunities to make up missed work.

19. Postsecondary Accommodations for Disability Disclosure

In higher education, students must disclose their disability to receive accommodations. Schools are obligated to keep this information confidential and provide necessary support.

20. Parental Rights and Advocacy

Parents of students with disabilities have the right to:

- Participate in educational planning and decision-making.
- Request evaluations or re-evaluations for special education services.
- Challenge decisions through due process hearings or mediation.

By addressing these circumstances, schools and institutions can ensure that students with disabilities receive the support they need to succeed academically and participate fully in their educational communities.

How to Advocate for Your Rights

Advocacy is critical in ensuring that your needs are met and your rights are respected.

Be Proactive

- **Know Your Rights:** Educate yourself about the ADA, Section 504, and IDEA to understand what schools must provide.
- **Document Everything:** Keep detailed records of evaluations, meetings, correspondence, and incidents.

Communicate Effectively

- Write clear, concise letters or emails when requesting accommodations or addressing issues.

- Attend meetings prepared with supporting documents and specific requests.
- Practice calm but assertive communication during disputes.

Understand Dispute Resolution Processes

If you face resistance, consider these steps:

- **Request Mediation:** A neutral third party can help resolve disagreements.
- **File a Complaint with the OCR:** The OCR investigates claims of discrimination and enforces federal law.
- **Consider Legal Action:** In extreme cases, consult an attorney who specializes in education law.

Overcoming Common Challenges

Denial of Services

If accommodations are denied, ask for a written explanation. Review the denial for errors or omissions and provide additional evidence if necessary.

Bullying and Harassment

Bullying based on disability is a violation of federal law. Report incidents immediately and document them thoroughly. If the school does not act, escalate the issue to state or federal authorities.

Teacher Resistance

When teachers resist implementing accommodations, address the issue with administrators. Remind them that accommodations are a legal requirement, not an option.

Resources for Support

- **Parent Training and Information Centers (PTIs):** Offer guidance for navigating special education systems.
- **WrightsLaw (wrightslaw.com):** Provides legal information on education rights.
- **Disability Rights Organizations:** Groups like the National Disability Rights Network (NDRN) offer advocacy services.

Examples of Disability Discrimination in Education

Disability discrimination in education occurs when students with disabilities are denied equal access, accommodations, or treated unfairly compared to their peers. Below are examples highlighting common forms of discrimination and how they violate the law.

1. Denied Access to Inclusive Classrooms

Scenario: A first-grade student with cerebral palsy, Emma, uses a wheelchair and excels academically. Her parents request that she be included in a general education classroom with her peers. However, the school insists on placing Emma in a separate classroom for students with physical disabilities, despite her ability to participate in the standard curriculum.

Discrimination: Denial of placement in the least restrictive environment, as required under the Individuals with Disabilities Education Act (IDEA).

2. Refusal to Provide Testing Accommodations

Scenario: Noah, a high school junior with dyslexia, requires extended time on tests and access to text-to-speech technology. Despite having a 504 Plan that specifies these accommodations, his math teacher refuses to implement them, arguing that it gives Noah an "unfair advantage."

Discrimination: Failure to implement reasonable accommodations, violating Section 504 of the Rehabilitation Act and the Americans with Disabilities Act (ADA).

3. Lack of Accessible Facilities

Scenario: A university student, Jacob, uses a motorized wheelchair. The lecture halls for his courses are located in an older building without elevators or ramps. Despite Jacob's repeated requests, the university delays relocating his classes to an accessible building.

Discrimination: Failure to provide physical access, violating the ADA and Section 504 requirements for post-secondary institutions.

---

4. Exclusion from Field Trips and Extracurricular Activities

Scenario: Sophia, a middle school student with autism, is excluded from a field trip to a museum because the teacher believes her behavior might disrupt the group. Her parents offer to provide a one-on-one aide, but the school denies their request.

Discrimination: Exclusion from extracurricular activities due to a disability, violating the ADA and Section 504.

---

5. Failure to Provide Assistive Technology

Scenario: Mia, a student with visual impairments, requires a screen reader to access her online coursework. The school provides standard laptops but refuses to accommodate her request for assistive software, citing budget constraints.

Discrimination: Denial of reasonable accommodations necessary for access to education, violating Section 504 and the ADA.

---

6. Bullying and Harassment Due to a Disability

Scenario: Ethan, a high school student with Tourette Syndrome, experiences frequent bullying from classmates, who mimic his tics and make cruel comments. The school dismisses his complaints as "kids being kids" and takes no action to address the harassment.

Discrimination: Failure to address disability-based harassment, violating the ADA and Title IX if the harassment impacts Ethan's education.

7. Retaliation for Advocating for Accommodations

Scenario: Sarah, a college student with ADHD, requests extended deadlines for her assignments through the school's disability services. After her professor reluctantly agrees, they begin criticizing her work harshly and marking her assignments down for minor errors.

Discrimination: Retaliation for requesting accommodations, violating the ADA and Section 504.

8. Failure to Recognize Invisible Disabilities

Scenario: Carlos, a student with an anxiety disorder, requests permission to take exams in a quiet room to reduce stress. His teacher denies the request, claiming Carlos does not "look disabled" and should "just deal with it like everyone else."

Discrimination: Disregard for invisible disabilities and denial of reasonable accommodations, violating the ADA and Section 504.

9. Denial of Service Animals

Scenario: Lily, a college student with PTSD, relies on a trained service dog for emotional support and to alert her to anxiety triggers. The university denies her request to bring the dog into classrooms, citing an outdated policy banning animals.

Discrimination: Refusal to allow a service animal, violating the ADA and Section 504 requirements for reasonable accommodations.

10. Unequal Discipline Policies

Scenario: Marcus, an elementary school student with ADHD, struggles to sit still during long lessons. When he gets up to move around the classroom, his teacher sends him to the principal's office and suspends him. However, other students without disabilities who act out are given warnings instead of punishment.

Discrimination: Unequal application of discipline policies, violating the ADA and Section 504's requirement for equitable treatment.

Each of these scenarios demonstrates how disability discrimination can manifest in educational settings. If you or someone you know faces similar situations, remember that federal laws like the ADA, Section 504, and IDEA protect against such unfair treatment. Advocate for your rights by documenting incidents, working with school officials, and seeking legal or advocacy support if necessary.

Empowering Yourself Through Advocacy

Education is a powerful tool, and your rights in this space are non-negotiable. By understanding the laws, advocating for accommodations, and standing firm in the face of challenges, you can ensure equitable access to education for yourself or your loved ones. Remember, fighting for your educational rights is not just about today—it's about creating a better, more inclusive future.

Chapter 4: Your Rights in Employment

For individuals with disabilities, employment is more than just a means of financial support—it's a source of personal fulfillment, social connection, and independence. Yet, all too often, people with disabilities face barriers that prevent them from fully participating in the workforce, whether it's discriminatory hiring practices, inaccessible workplaces, or a lack of understanding about reasonable accommodations. The **Americans with Disabilities Act (ADA)** provides vital protections, ensuring that individuals with disabilities have the right to pursue meaningful work and succeed in their careers. This chapter will help you understand your rights in the workplace, how to request accommodations, and what steps to take if you encounter discrimination.

ADA Protections in the Workplace

Employment Discrimination

Discrimination in the workplace is one of the most pervasive barriers to success for individuals with disabilities. The **ADA** prohibits discrimination against qualified individuals with disabilities in all aspects of employment, ensuring that you have equal access to job opportunities, promotions, training, and benefits. The following are key areas where the ADA provides protection:

- **Hiring and Firing:** Employers cannot make decisions about hiring or firing based on a disability. This means that even if a job applicant has a disability, they must be considered for the position based on their qualifications, not their condition. Similarly, if you're already employed, your disability cannot be the sole reason for termination unless it directly impacts your ability to perform essential job functions.

- **Promotions and Job Assignments:** The ADA ensures that you are given equal consideration for promotions and job assignments. Employers are not allowed to make decisions about job advancement based on disability-related assumptions, and any restrictions on promotions must be related to job performance, not your disability.

- **Compensation and Benefits:** The ADA ensures that you receive the same pay and benefits as other employees in similar positions, even if you require accommodations to perform your job. Employers cannot reduce your pay or benefits simply because of a disability.

- **Training and Development:** The ADA mandates that you have the same access to job-related training and development opportunities as other employees. Employers are prohibited from excluding you from these opportunities based on disability.

Reasonable Accommodations

Reasonable accommodations are adjustments made to the work environment or job duties to ensure that employees with disabilities can perform their jobs effectively. The ADA requires employers to provide accommodations, unless doing so would cause undue hardship. Here are common examples of reasonable accommodations:

- **Modification of Work Hours or Schedule:** Employers must allow flexible work hours, part-time schedules, or other scheduling accommodations if your disability makes traditional work hours difficult. This could be necessary for medical appointments, therapy sessions, or managing symptoms of your disability.

- **Job Restructuring or Reassignment of Tasks:** If there are certain tasks that are too physically demanding or mentally taxing due to your disability, employers must consider reassigning these tasks to others, or restructuring the job so that you can complete it without difficulty. For example, if you have mobility issues, you might be reassigned to a desk job instead of a position that requires standing for long periods.

- **Physical Accessibility Modifications:** This includes installing ramps, adjusting office furniture for wheelchair access, or providing assistive technology such as voice-activated software or screen readers. The goal is to make sure that you have the same ability to perform your job as other employees.

- **Assistive Technologies:** Employers are required to provide technologies that support your ability to complete job tasks, such as hearing aids, screen magnifiers, or special keyboards. These tools enable you to work effectively, ensuring that you have equal access to perform job functions.

Employers must also ensure that these accommodations are not just provided, but tailored to your specific needs. Reasonable accommodations may look different depending on the nature of your disability and the specific demands of your job.

Job-Related Protections

The ADA ensures that you are evaluated based on your actual job performance and not assumptions about your disability. Too often, people with disabilities face unconscious bias, where employers make decisions about their abilities based on stereotypes rather than objective criteria. The ADA helps address this by ensuring:

- **Objective Evaluation:** Employers are required to evaluate your performance based on the essential duties of your job, not on preconceived ideas about your abilities or limitations. If an employer assumes you cannot perform certain tasks based on your disability, they are violating your rights.

- **Clear Job Descriptions:** Employers must have clear and accurate job descriptions that outline essential functions, allowing both you and your employer to determine what accommodations might be necessary.

- **Disability-Related Inquiries:** Employers cannot ask for medical information or conduct disability-related inquiries unless it is directly related to your ability to perform essential job functions. If your disability doesn't affect your work, they are not entitled to ask you about it.

Requesting Accommodations

How to Request Accommodations

The process of requesting accommodations can sometimes feel intimidating, but knowing your rights and how to navigate the process can make it much smoother. Here are the steps for requesting accommodations under the ADA:

1. **Identify the Need for Accommodation:** The first step is to recognize areas in your work life where your disability may interfere with your job performance. This might include difficulties with mobility, communication, vision, or mental health. Understanding your needs will help you articulate them to your employer.

2. **Make the Request in Writing:** Although you may make the request orally, it is often a good idea to submit it in writing. This helps clarify your request and creates a record of your communication. Your written request should describe the nature of your disability and the accommodations you believe are necessary to perform the essential functions of your job.

3. **Provide Sufficient Information:** You do not have to disclose specific details about your medical condition, but you should provide enough information for your employer to understand your need for accommodation. You may also need to provide a letter from a healthcare provider that supports your request for accommodations.

4. **Be Specific About the Type of Accommodation:** Be clear about the specific accommodation(s) you need. For example, if you need a modified work schedule, specify the hours you require. If you need a specialized chair or desk, describe the type of equipment you need.

Interactive Process

Once your request is submitted, your employer is legally required to engage in an **interactive process** to discuss your needs and explore potential accommodations. Here's what that process looks like:

- **Employer's Responsibility:** Your employer must respond to your request for accommodation in a timely manner, and they should be open to working with you to find a solution. If your employer doesn't initiate a conversation or doesn't attempt to accommodate your needs, they are violating your rights.

- **Collaborative Problem-Solving:** This is a two-way conversation. Your employer will likely want to know more about how your disability impacts your job and what accommodations will help. The goal is to come to a mutually agreeable solution, one that meets your needs while not placing an undue burden on your employer.

- **Flexibility in Finding Solutions:** Accommodations don't have to be exactly what you requested, but they must enable you to do your job effectively. Employers can suggest alternatives as long as they meet your needs and the employer's business requirements.

Special Laws in Employment for Individuals with Disabilities

There are several disability-related special circumstances in employment that employers and employees should be aware of under the Americans with Disabilities Act (ADA) and other related laws. These circumstances revolve around ensuring equal opportunities, reasonable accommodations, and protection from discrimination in the workplace. The following is a non-exhaustive list of key special circumstances:

1. **Reasonable Accommodations**

    Employers must provide reasonable accommodations to qualified employees or applicants with disabilities unless doing so would cause undue hardship. Examples include:

    - Adjusting work schedules or permitting telework.
    - Providing assistive technology or modifying equipment.
    - Offering a quiet workspace for employees with sensory sensitivities (e.g., autism spectrum disorder).
    - Allowing breaks for medical needs, such as insulin monitoring for diabetes.

2. **Flexible Leave Policies**

    Employees with disabilities may need time off as a reasonable accommodation. This can include extended leave, intermittent leave, or a flexible schedule to attend medical appointments or manage treatment.

3. **Job Restructuring**

Employers may need to reassign non-essential duties to accommodate an employee's disability. For example, a warehouse worker with a physical disability may request relief from heavy lifting while still performing other critical job functions.

4. **Workplace Accessibility**

   Employers must ensure that the physical workspace is accessible to employees with disabilities. This includes:

   - Installing ramps, elevators, or automatic doors for wheelchair users.
   - Providing accessible restrooms and break areas.
   - Adapting desk heights or workstations.

5. **Assistive Technology**

   Providing tools or software that help employees perform their jobs is often necessary. Examples include screen readers for employees with visual impairments, voice recognition software, or specialized communication devices.

6. **Modified Hiring Processes**

   Employers must ensure that job applications, interviews, and hiring processes are accessible. For example:

   - Offering alternative formats for job applications (e.g., large print or online forms).
   - Allowing an applicant with a hearing impairment to bring an interpreter to an interview.
   - Conducting interviews in accessible locations.

7. **Disability-Related Harassment Protections**

   Employers must protect employees from harassment or a hostile work environment based on their disability. This includes addressing inappropriate comments, exclusion, or other forms of discriminatory treatment.

8. **Protection from Retaliation**

   Employees with disabilities are protected from retaliation if they assert their rights, such as requesting accommodations, filing a complaint, or participating in an investigation related to disability discrimination.

9. **Emergency Evacuation Plans**

   Employers must consider the needs of employees with disabilities when developing emergency plans. For example:
   - Providing visual alarms for employees who are deaf or hard of hearing.
   - Offering assistance or evacuation devices for employees with mobility impairments.

10. **Reassignment to a Vacant Position**

    If an employee can no longer perform the essential functions of their current position, even with accommodations, employers may need to reassign them to a vacant position for which they are qualified.

11. **Leave as an Accommodation**

    Employees with disabilities may request additional leave beyond what the employer offers as a standard benefit (e.g., under FMLA) if it enables them to recover or manage their disability. This must be considered unless it imposes an undue hardship.

12. **Disclosure and Confidentiality**

    Employees are not required to disclose their disability unless they are requesting accommodations. If disclosed, employers must keep this information confidential and share it only on a need-to-know basis.

13. **Service and Emotional Support Animals in the Workplace**

    While the ADA does not explicitly address emotional support animals in workplaces, employers may need to consider allowing service animals or emotional support animals as a reasonable accommodation under certain circumstances.

14. **Accommodations for Invisible Disabilities**

    Employees with invisible disabilities (e.g., mental health conditions, chronic illnesses) may require accommodations such as:

    - Flexible scheduling.
    - Reduced sensory input in the workplace.
    - Job coaching or mentoring programs.

15. **Reinstatement After Medical Leave**

    Employees with disabilities are entitled to return to their positions after medical leave, provided they can perform the essential functions of the job, with or without accommodations.

16. **Workplace Policies and Disability-Related Exceptions**

    Employers may need to adjust policies for employees with disabilities. Examples include:

    - Adjusting attendance policies for individuals who need time off for treatment.
    - Allowing food or drink at workstations for employees with diabetes.
    - Permitting frequent breaks for individuals with certain conditions, like multiple sclerosis.

17. **Disability-Related Misconduct**

    If an employee's disability results in behavior that violates workplace policies (e.g., outbursts related to a mental health condition), employers must evaluate whether reasonable accommodations could address the issue before taking disciplinary action.

18. **Support During the Transition to Work**

Employees returning to work after acquiring a disability or undergoing treatment may need transitional accommodations, such as part-time hours, gradual workload increases, or additional support during the adjustment period.

19. **Performance and Disability Accommodations**

    Employees with disabilities must still meet performance standards, but employers may need to provide accommodations to help them achieve those standards.

By addressing these circumstances, employers can create inclusive workplaces while ensuring compliance with the ADA and fostering a supportive environment for employees with disabilities.

Recognizing Discrimination

Discrimination can happen in many forms in the workplace. Recognizing the signs is key to protecting your rights. Some signs of workplace discrimination include:

- **Denial of Accommodations:** If your employer refuses to provide reasonable accommodations or delays responding to your request without a valid reason, this is a violation of the ADA.

- **Exclusion from Opportunities:** If you're not considered for training, promotions, or special projects because of your disability, it may be discriminatory.

- **Increased Scrutiny or Bias:** If you're subjected to more scrutiny or unfair treatment compared to your coworkers due to your disability, this could be a form of discrimination.

- **Harassment or Hostility:** If you face harassment, mocking, or other negative behaviors related to your disability, this constitutes discrimination.

Addressing Issues

If you experience discrimination in the workplace, it's important to address it as soon as possible:

- **Document the Discriminatory Acts:** Keep a record of every discriminatory incident, including dates, times, locations, and any individuals involved. This will be critical if you decide to take formal action.

- **Speak with Your Employer:** In many cases, issues can be resolved by having an open and respectful conversation with your employer or HR. Explain the situation, provide documentation if necessary, and ask for an explanation of why the discrimination occurred.

- **File a Formal Complaint:** If informal solutions don't work, you can file a complaint with the **Equal Employment Opportunity Commission (EEOC)**. The EEOC investigates workplace discrimination and enforces ADA rights. Filing a complaint with the EEOC must be done within 180 days of the discriminatory act.

Retaliation

The ADA protects you from retaliation. If you file a complaint or request accommodations and your employer retaliates against you in any way—such as firing you, reducing your hours, or changing your job duties—it's illegal. You are entitled to:

- **Protection Against Retaliation:** If you believe your employer is retaliating against you for asserting your rights, you can file a retaliation claim with the EEOC or seek legal advice.

- **Understand Your Rights:** Retaliation can include negative job performance evaluations, denial of promotions, or changes to your job duties that weren't related to job performance. If retaliation occurs, it is important to document and report it immediately.

Examples of Disability Discrimination in Employment

Denied Accommodations

1. Denied Ergonomic Workspace (Physical Disability)

Maria, an administrative assistant with chronic back pain due to scoliosis, requests an ergonomic chair and a height-adjustable desk to reduce strain while working. Despite her doctor's recommendation and medical documentation, her manager denies the request, saying the company cannot afford such equipment. This decision forces Maria to work in discomfort, exacerbating her condition.

Discrimination: Denial of reasonable accommodation under the ADA.

Explanation: Employers are obligated to provide necessary workplace adjustments to employees with physical disabilities when reasonable.

2. Denied Telework for PTSD (Mental Health Disability)

Ryan, a graphic designer with post-traumatic stress disorder (PTSD), finds it difficult to work in a crowded office due to his triggers. He requests to work from home part-time as an accommodation. His employer denies the request, claiming that the role requires an office presence, even though other employees are allowed remote work for non-disability reasons.

Discrimination: Denial of reasonable accommodation under the ADA.

Explanation: Refusing remote work for an employee with PTSD while offering it to others may constitute discrimination if the accommodation is feasible.

3. Denied Extended Training Time (Neurodivergent Disability)

Eli, a warehouse worker with dyslexia, requires additional time to complete written training assessments. Despite informing his supervisor and providing documentation, Eli's request is denied, and he is penalized for failing to complete the training on time.

Discrimination: Denial of reasonable accommodation under the ADA.

Explanation: Employers must provide accommodations, like extended time, to employees with learning disabilities to ensure equal access to training and resources.

Harassment

4. Mocking Physical Limitations (Physical Disability)

Jack, a delivery driver who uses a prosthetic leg, faces daily teasing from coworkers, who call him names like "Tin Man" and make jokes about his pace. Despite reporting the harassment to HR, the behavior continues, making Jack feel isolated and devalued.

Discrimination: Harassment based on disability under the ADA.

Explanation: Employers are required to address and prevent harassment of employees with physical disabilities.

5. Targeted Bullying for Bipolar Disorder (Mental Health Disability)

Emily, a customer service representative with bipolar disorder, is open about her condition to reduce stigma. However, coworkers frequently joke about her "mood swings," claiming she's unpredictable and unreliable. When Emily confronts them, they dismiss it as harmless humor.

Discrimination: Harassment based on disability under the ADA.

Explanation: Mocking or stigmatizing an employee's mental health condition creates a hostile work environment and violates the ADA.

6. Harassment for Sensory Needs (Neurodivergent Disability)

Oliver, who has sensory processing disorder, requests noise-canceling headphones to reduce office distractions. Some colleagues begin tapping loudly near him and intentionally creating noise to provoke a reaction, making him feel unwelcome and unsupported.

Discrimination: Harassment based on disability under the ADA.

Explanation: Employers must intervene to prevent harassment targeting an employee's sensory needs.

Retaliation

7. Retaliation After Requesting Accessible Parking (Physical Disability)

Megan, who uses a wheelchair, requests an accessible parking space closer to the building entrance. After the request is approved, her supervisor begins scrutinizing her work more harshly and excludes her from team projects, making her feel targeted.

Discrimination: Retaliation under the ADA.
Explanation: Retaliating against an employee for requesting accommodations, such as accessible parking, is prohibited by the ADA.

8. Retaliation After Disclosing Anxiety (Mental Health Disability)

Jordan, a technical writer with generalized anxiety disorder, requests occasional time off to attend therapy. Following this disclosure, his supervisor assigns him high-pressure tasks with unrealistic deadlines, knowing these worsen his anxiety.

Discrimination: Retaliation under the ADA.
Explanation: Increasing workload or creating a stressful environment after a disclosure violates ADA protections against retaliation.

9. Retaliation for Neurodivergent Needs

Chloe, an IT specialist with autism, requests a quieter workspace to reduce sensory overload. After her request, she is reassigned to less desirable projects and excluded from important meetings, limiting her career growth.

Discrimination: Retaliation under the ADA.
Explanation: Penalizing employees for requesting accommodations, such as a sensory-friendly workspace, is illegal under the ADA.

Failure to Hire

10. Denial Due to Mobility Limitations (Physical Disability)

Daniel, who uses crutches, applies for a sales role that involves occasional travel. During the interview, the manager questions how Daniel would manage travel and suggests he might not be a good "fit" for the role. Despite Daniel being qualified, he is not hired.

Discrimination: Failure to hire based on disability under the ADA.

Explanation: Employers cannot make hiring decisions based on assumptions about a candidate's disability.

11. Failure to Hire for PTSD Disclosure (Mental Health Disability)

Renee, a veteran with PTSD, applies for a position as a paralegal. When she discloses her condition during the interview and explains her coping strategies, the interviewer becomes dismissive. Renee later learns that the employer hired someone less qualified.

Discrimination: Failure to hire based on disability under the ADA.

Explanation: Employers must not use a mental health condition as a factor in hiring decisions.

12. Rejection for Autism (Neurodivergent Disability)

Sam, who is on the autism spectrum, applies for an engineering role and requests a structured interview process to help him focus. Despite his qualifications, Sam is not selected, and feedback reveals the employer was concerned about his "fit with company culture."

Discrimination: Failure to hire based on disability under the ADA.

Explanation: Denying employment due to a neurodivergent condition or requested accommodations is discriminatory.

Failure to Promote

13. Denial Due to Vision Impairment (Physical Disability)

Linda, an accountant with low vision, applies for a managerial role. Despite meeting all qualifications and excelling in her role, she is passed over for a less experienced colleague. Linda's supervisor privately mentions concerns about her ability to "lead with her limitations."

Discrimination: Failure to promote based on disability under the ADA.

Explanation: Decisions about promotions must be based on merit, not unfounded assumptions about physical disabilities.

14. Passed Over for Mental Health Diagnosis

Victor, a legal assistant with depression, applies for a supervisory role. Despite his high performance, he is told the position requires "emotional resilience" and is given to another candidate.

Discrimination: Failure to promote based on disability under the ADA.
Explanation: Mental health conditions should not disqualify employees from promotions when they meet job qualifications.

15. Failure to Promote Due to ADHD

Nina, a teacher with ADHD, applies for a leadership position. Despite her strong record, her supervisor says she might lack the "focus" required for the role. Nina suspects her ADHD was unfairly considered.

Discrimination: Failure to promote based on disability under the ADA.
Explanation: Employers cannot make biased decisions based on a neurodivergent condition.

Highlighting the reality of neurodivergence and sensory disabilities in the workplace is essential because individuals with these conditions make up a crucial part of both the workforce and the population. While they bring valuable skills and unique perspectives, they often face challenges like sensory sensitivities and social interaction difficulties. These differences are frequently misunderstood, leading to discrimination and missed opportunities. By raising awareness and fostering inclusivity, we can ensure neurodivergent individuals receive the support they need to succeed, creating a more equitable and productive work environment for all.

These examples underscore the need for increased understanding and proactive measures to support neurodivergent and sensory-disabled employees. It is crucial for employers to recognize the challenges these individuals face and to create inclusive, accommodating environments that allow them to thrive. By addressing discrimination and fostering a workplace that values all abilities, organizations can unlock the full potential of their diverse workforce.

Pregnancy Discrimination

In some jurisdictions, pregnancy is considered a disability, which means that pregnant workers are entitled to reasonable accommodations under laws similar to those that protect employees with other disabilities. The **Pregnant Workers Fairness Act (PWFA)**, passed in 2022, is a crucial piece of legislation that ensures pregnant employees are provided with necessary accommodations, such as modified duties, flexible work schedules, or additional breaks, when pregnancy-related limitations arise. This act builds on the protections provided by the **Pregnancy Discrimination Act (PDA)**, which prohibits discrimination based on pregnancy, childbirth, or related medical conditions.

Under the PWFA, employers are required to make accommodations for workers who experience pregnancy-related limitations, just as they would for employees with disabilities. This legislation ensures that pregnant employees can continue working without jeopardizing their health or the safety of their pregnancies. It also clarifies that employers must treat pregnancy-related conditions with the same consideration as other temporary disabilities, offering protections against discrimination and ensuring equal access to reasonable accommodations.

For example, a pregnant worker may request light-duty work or more frequent breaks due to medical needs arising from pregnancy. If such accommodations are denied, it could constitute discrimination under the **Pregnant Workers Fairness Act**, ensuring that pregnant employees receive the same protections as other workers with temporary disabilities.

- **Denied Temporary Light Duty Due to Pregnancy**

Sarah, a warehouse worker who is six months pregnant, requests a temporary light-duty assignment to avoid lifting heavy boxes and standing for long periods, which her doctor has recommended. Despite her excellent performance record, her supervisor denies the request, stating that the company doesn't offer light-duty work to anyone, regardless of medical need. Sarah is told she must continue her regular duties, and when she struggles, she is written up for performance issues.

Discrimination: Denial of reasonable accommodation under the PDA.

Explanation: Pregnant employees are entitled to reasonable accommodations for pregnancy-related conditions that affect their ability to work, similar to accommodations provided for other disabilities. Denying light-duty work when requested for health reasons constitutes pregnancy discrimination.

- **Harassment Due to Pregnancy**

Emily, a senior project manager, announces her pregnancy and soon begins experiencing subtle harassment from her colleagues. They make comments about her ability to handle the workload while pregnant, with some colleagues saying she will be too distracted to manage her responsibilities. In meetings, she is excluded from certain discussions, and her role is gradually diminished. When Emily complains to HR, she is told that "it's just because everyone is concerned" and that "things will be easier after the baby comes."

Discrimination: Harassment based on pregnancy under the PDA.
Explanation: Harassment due to pregnancy or assumptions about a pregnant employee's abilities is a form of discrimination. Employers must ensure that employees are treated fairly, regardless of pregnancy, and intervene when inappropriate behavior occurs.

- **Exclusion from Promotions Due to Pregnancy**

Monica, a marketing executive, is expecting her first child and is excited about a promotion opportunity that has been discussed with her for months. When the promotion is awarded to a colleague, Monica is told that her "focus will likely shift after maternity leave," and the company needs someone who will be more "committed" long-term.

Despite her strong qualifications and years of experience, Monica suspects her pregnancy was a factor in the decision.

Discrimination: Failure to promote based on pregnancy under the PDA.
Explanation: Discriminating against an employee for being pregnant, or assuming that a pregnant employee won't be able to perform at the same level after maternity leave, violates the PDA. Employers must make promotion decisions based on qualifications and performance, not pregnancy status.

- **Denial of Flexible Schedule for Medical Appointments During Pregnancy**

Linda, a teacher, is in her second trimester and needs to attend frequent medical appointments related to her pregnancy. She requests a flexible schedule to accommodate these appointments, offering to make up missed work during her lunch break. Her supervisor denies the request, stating that the schedule is "non-negotiable" and that no one else gets accommodations for personal appointments. Linda is forced to take unpaid leave for her appointments, causing unnecessary financial strain.

Discrimination: Denial of reasonable accommodation under the PDA.
Explanation: Employers are required to offer reasonable accommodations for pregnancy-related medical conditions, such as flexible scheduling for appointments. Denying this request when it would not cause undue hardship to the employer constitutes discrimination.

- **Denied Temporary Light Duty Due to Pregnancy**

Sarah, a warehouse worker who is six months pregnant, requests a temporary light-duty assignment to avoid lifting heavy boxes and standing for long periods, which her doctor has recommended. Despite her excellent performance record, her supervisor denies the request, stating that the company doesn't offer light-duty work to anyone, regardless of medical need. Sarah is told she must continue her regular duties, and when she struggles, she is written up for performance issues.

Discrimination: Denial of reasonable accommodation under the **Pregnant Workers Fairness Act**.

Explanation: Under the PWFA, pregnant employees are entitled to reasonable accommodations for pregnancy-related conditions, including light-duty assignments. Denying these accommodations violates the law and puts undue strain on the employee.

- **Harassment Due to Pregnancy**

Emily, a senior project manager, announces her pregnancy and soon begins experiencing subtle harassment from her colleagues. They make comments about her ability to handle the workload while pregnant, with some colleagues saying she will be too distracted to manage her responsibilities. In meetings, she is excluded from certain discussions, and her role is gradually diminished. When Emily complains to HR, she is told that "it's just because everyone is concerned" and that "things will be easier after the baby comes."

Discrimination: Harassment based on pregnancy under the **Pregnant Workers Fairness Act**.

Explanation: Harassment due to pregnancy or assumptions about a pregnant employee's abilities is discriminatory. The PWFA requires employers to create a respectful environment for all employees, including pregnant workers.

Conclusion:

All of these scenarios provide real-world examples of how disability discrimination can manifest in the workplace, affecting various individuals with different disabilities, including physical, mental, and neurodivergent conditions. Understanding and recognizing these forms of discrimination is crucial for employees with disabilities to advocate for their rights and ensure that their working conditions are fair and equitable.

Summary

In this chapter, we've covered key information about your rights in the workplace under the ADA, including protections against discrimination, how to request accommodations, and what to do if you face discrimination. It's crucial to know that your disability does not define your ability to succeed in your job. Employers are required to provide reasonable accommodations and ensure equal treatment. If you encounter discrimination, you have the right to challenge it and seek justice.

Chapter 5: Access to Public Services and Spaces

Access to public services and spaces is a fundamental right that ensures individuals, regardless of disabilities, can fully participate in society. This chapter covers the various legal rights people with disabilities have regarding public accommodations and services. It explores how the law ensures accessibility in public settings and outlines the steps to take when access is denied or insufficient. Understanding how to advocate for yourself and others is critical to upholding these rights and fostering an inclusive community.

Public Accommodations

Legal Rights: Your Right to Access Facilities, Transportation, and Services in Public Spaces

The Americans with Disabilities Act (ADA) mandates that individuals with disabilities must have equal access to public accommodations. Public accommodations refer to a wide range of facilities that provide goods or services to the general public, including but not limited to restaurants, theaters, hotels, retail stores, medical offices, and transportation systems.

The ADA prohibits discrimination on the basis of disability in these places. Businesses and public entities are required to ensure that their facilities are accessible to all individuals, which includes removing architectural barriers or providing accessible alternatives to ensure equal access to services. For instance, wheelchair-accessible ramps, service animal policies, and clear signage in accessible formats are all part of the obligation that businesses have to provide equitable access.

- **Restaurants and Retail Stores**: These must provide accessible paths for individuals using wheelchairs or other mobility devices. This includes ensuring that the seating, counters, and aisles are navigable.

- **Hotels and Lodging**: Hotels must provide accessible rooms, bathrooms, and other necessary facilities for individuals with disabilities. This includes features like grab bars, visual and auditory alarms, and wide doorways.

- **Transportation**: Public transportation services, including buses, trains, and taxis, must be accessible to individuals with disabilities. This includes features like accessible ramps, priority seating, and audible announcements.

In addition to physical access, the ADA also mandates that businesses and public services offer communication aids and services, including providing sign language interpreters or assistive listening devices where necessary.

Accessibility Features: Understanding What Constitutes an Accessible Public Space

An accessible public space must be designed or retrofitted to meet specific standards that accommodate individuals with disabilities. These standards ensure that people with mobility, vision, hearing, or other impairments can fully participate in activities within the space. Some essential accessibility features include:

- **Ramps**: Ramps are required at entrances where stairs are present to allow wheelchair users, those with strollers, or individuals with other mobility issues to access buildings. The slope of the ramp must meet specific guidelines to ensure it is safe and usable for everyone.

- **Elevators**: Multi-story buildings must be equipped with elevators that are fully accessible. This includes wide doors, low-control buttons that are easy to reach, tactile markings for the visually impaired, and audio announcements of floor numbers.

- **Parking**: Accessible parking spaces must be provided near entrances to public facilities. These spaces are wider than standard parking spots to accommodate mobility devices, and they must be clearly marked with signs indicating their purpose.

- **Public Restrooms**: Accessible restrooms should have sufficient space to maneuver a wheelchair and include features such as grab bars, sinks at the correct height, and stalls large enough for a wheelchair.

- **Service Counters and Communication**: Public service counters must be at a height that allows individuals with disabilities to approach easily. Public spaces must also provide communication accommodations such as sign language interpreters or written materials for those who are deaf or hard of hearing.

Special Laws in Public Accommodations and Public Spaces

Disability-related special circumstances in public accommodations and public spaces are primarily addressed under the **Americans with Disabilities Act (ADA)**. These regulations ensure that individuals with disabilities have equal access to facilities, services, and opportunities in public and private spaces that are open to the public. Below is an overview of some of these special circumstances:

1. Physical Accessibility Requirements

Public accommodations must ensure their facilities are physically accessible to individuals with disabilities. This includes:

- Ramps, elevators, or lifts to provide access to buildings and upper floors.
- Accessible restrooms with grab bars and wide stalls.
- Automatic or easy-to-open doors.
- Designated accessible parking spaces near building entrances.
- Tactile signs for individuals with visual impairments.

2. Reasonable Modifications to Policies and Procedures

Businesses and public facilities must make reasonable changes to policies to accommodate individuals with disabilities, such as:

- Allowing service animals in spaces where pets are otherwise prohibited.
- Permitting individuals with disabilities to bring personal aids, like oxygen tanks or mobility devices.

3. Effective Communication

Public accommodations must ensure effective communication with individuals with disabilities. This includes providing:

- Auxiliary aids and services, such as sign language interpreters, captions, or communication devices.

- Accessible formats for written materials, such as Braille, large print, or audio recordings.
- Real-time captioning during events or public meetings.

4. Service Animals

Individuals with disabilities are allowed to bring service animals to public spaces, even where pets are prohibited.

- The service animal must be trained to perform tasks related to the individual's disability.
- Businesses may only ask whether the animal is a service animal and what tasks it performs but cannot request proof or certification.

5. Access to Public Transportation

Public transportation systems, including buses, trains, and subways, must be accessible to individuals with disabilities. Requirements include:

- Lifts or ramps for boarding.
- Priority seating for individuals with disabilities.
- Accessible ticketing systems and platforms.

6. Emergency Evacuation Plans

Public spaces must develop and communicate emergency evacuation plans that include accommodations for individuals with disabilities, such as:

- Audible and visual alarms.
- Staff trained to assist individuals with mobility challenges during evacuations.

7. Equal Access to Goods and Services

Businesses and public facilities must ensure individuals with disabilities can access goods and services on an equal basis. Examples include:

- Rearranging furniture or displays in stores to accommodate wheelchairs.

- Providing curbside service for individuals unable to navigate store interiors.

8. Accessibility of Public Events

Event organizers must ensure public events are inclusive for individuals with disabilities by providing:

- Accessible seating and viewing areas.
- Transportation to and from venues that accommodate mobility devices.
- ASL interpreters, live captioning, or assistive listening devices during presentations.

9. Digital Accessibility

Websites and online services operated by public accommodations must be accessible to individuals with disabilities, including those with:

- Screen reader compatibility for individuals with visual impairments.
- Captioned videos for individuals with hearing impairments.
- Keyboard navigation for individuals with mobility impairments.

10. Accommodations in Hotels and Lodging

Hotels and similar facilities must offer accessible accommodations, such as:

- Rooms with roll-in showers, grab bars, and wider doorways.
- Accessible check-in counters.
- Features for individuals with hearing impairments, such as visual alarms and TTY devices.

11. Access to Recreational Facilities

Recreational facilities, including parks, pools, and gyms, must be accessible to individuals with disabilities. Examples include:

- Accessible playground equipment.
- Pool lifts or zero-entry pools for individuals with mobility impairments.

- Trails and pathways designed for wheelchair access.

12. Public Restrooms

Public restrooms must meet ADA standards for accessibility, such as:

- Wide stalls with grab bars.
- Accessible sinks and hand dryers at appropriate heights.

13. Access to Healthcare Facilities

Hospitals, clinics, and other healthcare facilities must ensure accessibility for individuals with disabilities, including:

- Examination tables and diagnostic equipment that accommodate mobility devices.
- Sign language interpreters or assistive technology during appointments.
- Flexible scheduling for patients with chronic illnesses or disabilities.

14. Exemptions for Religious Organizations

While religious organizations and private clubs are generally exempt from the ADA, they are encouraged to provide accessibility to individuals with disabilities to promote inclusion.

15. Temporary Structures and Events

Temporary structures like pop-up shops, outdoor markets, or festivals must provide accessibility features, such as:

- Portable ramps or lifts.
- Accessible portable restrooms.

16. Accessible Voting Locations

Polling places must be accessible to individuals with disabilities, including:

- Ballot machines designed for individuals with visual or mobility impairments.

- Accessible entrances and parking at voting locations.

17. Disability-Related Flexibility in Rules

Public spaces may need to waive certain rules or policies to accommodate individuals with disabilities. Examples include:

- Allowing individuals with sensory disabilities (e.g., autism) to wear noise-canceling headphones.
- Granting additional time for completing tasks or using facilities.

18. Accessible Sports and Fitness Facilities

Gyms, stadiums, and fitness centers must provide accessibility, such as:

- Adaptive fitness equipment.
- Accessible locker rooms and showers.
- Wheelchair-accessible seating in stadiums.

19. Right to File Complaints

Individuals with disabilities can file complaints with the Department of Justice or local authorities if public accommodations or spaces fail to meet ADA standards.

By addressing these circumstances, public accommodations and public spaces can ensure they are inclusive and accessible to individuals with disabilities, enabling equal participation and opportunity in community life.

Disability Discrimination in Public Accommodations

Public accommodations, which include private businesses and services open to the public (such as restaurants, hotels, theaters, and stores), are required by law to provide equal access to individuals with disabilities. This is mandated by the **Americans with Disabilities Act (ADA)**, which ensures that individuals with disabilities are not excluded from participating in or benefiting from services, programs, or activities. However, disability discrimination can still occur, often in the form of inaccessibility, denial of services, or failure to provide reasonable accommodations. Below are expanded hypotheticals that showcase various ways in which public accommodations may fail to comply with the law, categorized by the type of violation.

Inaccessible Restaurant Facilities

Category: Inaccessibility in Public Spaces

Scenario:
Jessica, a woman who uses a wheelchair, visits a popular downtown restaurant to meet her friends. When she arrives, she notices that the only entrance to the restaurant is up a flight of stairs. She approaches the restaurant staff, explaining that she uses a wheelchair and asking if there's an accessible entrance. The staff informs her that the building has been around for decades and they "don't have the budget" to create a ramp. Jessica is offered no alternative but to leave or be carried upstairs by her friends.

Discrimination: Denial of access due to an inaccessible physical space. The restaurant is required under the ADA to ensure that its facilities, including entrances, are accessible to individuals with mobility impairments, either through ramps or elevators.

Legal Recourse: Jessica can file a complaint with the Department of Justice (DOJ) or pursue legal action to compel the restaurant to make its space accessible.

Denied Accessible Hotel Room

Category: Denial of Accessible Features

Scenario:
Mark, who has a mobility impairment and uses a wheelchair, books a room at a popular hotel chain known for its accessible accommodations. Upon his arrival, the hotel desk clerk informs him that there are no accessible rooms available, even though he had confirmed the reservation in advance. The clerk offers him a regular room that is not wheelchair accessible, stating that the hotel is "fully booked" and they "don't have any other rooms."

Discrimination: Failure to provide a reserved accessible room. Hotels are required by the ADA to reserve accessible rooms for people with disabilities, and when one is reserved, the hotel must honor that reservation or offer a comparable accessible room.

Legal Recourse: Mark can file a complaint with the Department of Justice or a state agency that enforces public accommodation laws. He may also file a private lawsuit for violation of the ADA.

Autism Discrimination in a Movie Theater

Category: Discrimination Based on Disability

Scenario:
Michael, who is on the autism spectrum, loves going to the movies but often struggles with the loud sounds and bright visuals that can be overwhelming. He has contacted his local movie theater in advance to request accommodations such as reduced sound levels and dimmed lights for an upcoming film. The theater agrees to the request, but when he arrives, the accommodations are not made, and the staff is unaware of the arrangements. Michael asks the manager to adjust the sound and lighting as discussed, but the manager refuses, saying, "We can't make those changes just for one person." Michael is forced to leave, unable to enjoy the movie.

Discrimination: Denial of reasonable accommodation under the ADA. Public accommodations, like movie theaters, must provide adjustments to ensure people with disabilities can access services and participate on equal terms. Failing to fulfill agreed-upon accommodations is discriminatory.

Legal Recourse: Michael can file a complaint with the DOJ or the ADA enforcement body, seeking resolution and ensuring that accommodations are properly made in the future. He can also pursue legal action if the theater refuses to provide the agreed-upon adjustments for individuals with disabilities.

Inaccessible Parking at a Shopping Mall

Category: Inaccessible Facilities

Scenario:
Carlos, who uses a wheelchair, visits a local shopping mall to run errands. Upon arrival, all accessible parking spaces are taken, and there are no alternative accessible parking spots nearby. The nearest parking spaces are far from the mall entrance, and the walking paths to the entrance are poorly maintained and difficult to navigate in a wheelchair. Carlos is forced to park in a regular parking space, a long distance away, making it difficult for him to reach the entrance.

Discrimination: Failure to provide adequate accessible parking spaces and paths of travel to and from the building. Under the ADA, public accommodations must provide accessible parking spaces close to the entrance and ensure that paths of travel are free from obstacles and well-maintained.

Legal Recourse: Carlos can file a complaint with the DOJ or request corrective measures from the mall's management to improve accessibility.

Denied Service Due to Service Animal

Category: Discrimination Due to Disability-Related Assistance

Scenario:
Rachel, who is blind and uses a service dog, enters a coffee shop. When she tries to order her drink, the barista informs her that "no pets are allowed." Rachel explains that her dog is a service animal, not a pet, and that the ADA permits service animals in public accommodations. However, the barista refuses to serve her, saying, "We don't want dogs in here, service or not." Rachel attempts to speak with the manager, but the manager backs up the barista's decision.

Discrimination: Denial of service based on the presence of a service animal. Under the ADA, businesses must allow service animals to accompany individuals with disabilities, unless the animal poses a direct threat to health or safety.

Legal Recourse: Rachel can file a complaint with the DOJ or seek legal action against the coffee shop for refusal to serve her due to her service animal.

Inadequate Accessible Restroom at a Public Facility

Category: Inaccessibility of Restrooms

Scenario:
James, who uses a wheelchair, visits a government building to attend a public hearing. He finds the building's accessible restroom, but the door is too narrow to fit his wheelchair through, and it is impossible for him to enter the stall. There is no other accessible restroom in the building, and when James informs the building's staff, they say, "There's nothing we can do about it right now."

Discrimination: Failure to provide accessible restroom facilities, which is required by the ADA. Public accommodations are required to ensure that restroom facilities are accessible to all patrons, including individuals with mobility impairments.

Legal Recourse: James can file a complaint with the DOJ or take legal action against the public facility for failing to provide accessible restroom facilities.

Discriminatory Treatment in a Store Due to Disability

Category: Discriminatory Behavior by Staff

Scenario:
Anna, who has cerebral palsy and uses crutches, enters a department store to purchase some clothing. The sales associate immediately assumes she needs help, and proceeds to follow her around the store without asking if assistance is needed. When Anna expresses frustration and asks for help finding a specific item, the sales associate says, "You probably won't be able to carry that anyway."

Discrimination: Discriminatory behavior based on assumptions about a person's disability. Public accommodations must treat all individuals equally and avoid making assumptions about what a person can or cannot do due to their disability.

Legal Recourse: Anna can file a complaint with the DOJ or file a lawsuit against the store for discriminatory treatment under the ADA.

Inaccessible Fitness Center Equipment

Category: Inaccessible Services and Facilities

Scenario:
David, who has a spinal cord injury and uses a wheelchair, visits a local fitness center with the intention of working out. He asks the staff if the center has equipment designed for individuals with mobility impairments, and they tell him that they are unsure. David is told there is no accessible gym equipment and is unable to use the gym facilities.

Discrimination: Failure to provide accessible gym equipment and services. Fitness centers, like other public accommodations, are required to provide reasonable access to all individuals, including those with mobility impairments.

Legal Recourse: David can file a complaint with the DOJ or request modifications to the fitness center's equipment and policies.

Inaccessible Public Transportation

Category: Inaccessible Public Services

Scenario:
Maria, who uses a wheelchair, attempts to board a city bus. Upon arriving, she notices that the accessible ramp is broken, and the driver is unable to provide an alternative. The driver tells her that the next bus should have an accessible ramp, but Maria has an important appointment that she is now unable to attend.

Discrimination: Failure to provide accessible public transportation. Public transit systems are required to have accessible vehicles and must ensure that they are operational for individuals with mobility impairments.

Legal Recourse: Maria can file a complaint with the local transportation agency or with the Department of Transportation, which enforces accessibility standards for public transit.

Exclusion from a Public Event Due to Disability

Category: Exclusion from Public Services

Scenario:
Tom, who is deaf, attends a public conference being held at a convention center. When he arrives, he finds that none of the sessions offer sign language interpreters or captioning. Tom speaks to event organizers, who tell him that "no one else has requested those services" and that they "don't think it's necessary for this event." Tom is forced to leave without attending any of the sessions.

Discrimination: Failure to provide necessary accommodations for individuals with hearing impairments. Public events, including conferences, are required to provide communication access, such as sign language interpreters or captioning, when needed.

Legal Recourse: Tom can file a complaint with the DOJ or with the event organizers, requesting corrective measures and accommodations under the ADA.

These hypotheticals highlight the various forms of disability discrimination that can occur in public accommodations, from inaccessible facilities to denial of services or accommodations. Under the ADA, businesses and public services are required to ensure that people with disabilities have equal access to the services they provide. Understanding these rights, filing complaints, and seeking legal remedies are important steps in ensuring that individuals with disabilities can access public spaces and services without facing discrimination.

Conclusion

The right to access public services and spaces is crucial to ensuring that all individuals, regardless of ability, can participate fully in society. The ADA, IDEA, Section 504, and related laws have been put in place to ensure that public accommodations and educational institutions meet the needs of people with disabilities. However, these rights are only effective if individuals are aware of their legal protections and how to assert them when necessary.

By understanding the various ways that public services and spaces must be made accessible, and knowing the steps to take when access is denied, individuals with disabilities can better advocate for themselves. Whether filing a complaint, requesting accommodations, or seeking legal recourse, it's essential to stand up for your rights and ensure that you are treated with the respect and dignity you deserve.

Chapter 6: Housing Rights and Fair Housing

Fair Housing Act

The **Fair Housing Act (FHA)** is a pivotal piece of civil rights legislation that prohibits discrimination in the sale, rental, and financing of housing based on several protected classes, including disability. It ensures that individuals with disabilities have the same rights and access to housing as anyone else. This law mandates that housing providers make reasonable accommodations or modifications to allow disabled individuals to fully enjoy their homes and the associated services. The scope of this law is broad, covering public and private housing providers, including apartment complexes, single-family homes, rental agencies, real estate brokers, mortgage lenders, and housing-related insurance companies.

The protections under the Fair Housing Act extend to all aspects of housing, including access to facilities, services, and housing-related activities. It ensures that individuals with disabilities can live independently and participate in community life by preventing discrimination in housing based on their disability status.

Protections in Housing: Your Right to Rent or Purchase a Home Free from Disability Discrimination

Under the FHA, individuals with disabilities have the right to rent or purchase a home without facing discrimination based on their disability. Housing providers cannot refuse to rent or sell a property simply because an individual has a disability. They also cannot impose different or unfair terms or conditions on rental agreements, such as charging higher rent or requiring larger security deposits because of the individual's disability.

This right extends beyond the lease agreement itself. Housing providers must ensure that individuals with disabilities can fully access housing-related services, including amenities, parking spaces, and maintenance services, on the same terms as other tenants.

For instance, a landlord cannot refuse to lease an apartment to someone who uses a wheelchair or has a mental health condition. Additionally, a mortgage lender cannot refuse to approve a loan or increase interest rates simply because an applicant has a disability.

Reasonable Accommodations and Modifications

The **Fair Housing Act** requires housing providers to make **reasonable accommodations** and **modifications** for individuals with disabilities to ensure they have equal access to housing.

- **Reasonable Modifications**: This refers to physical changes made to the property itself, necessary for an individual with a disability to live there safely and comfortably. For example, a person with limited mobility may request the installation of a ramp or grab bars in the bathroom. The housing provider is required to allow these modifications at the tenant's expense, unless doing so would create an undue hardship for the provider.

- **Reasonable Accommodations**: These are changes or exceptions to the housing provider's policies, practices, or rules that allow a tenant with a disability to fully use and enjoy their dwelling. For example, a tenant who uses a service animal may request that the landlord waive a no-pet policy or allow an emotional support animal, even if the building has a no-pet rule. Another example might include a request for reserved parking closer to the building for someone with a disability.

It's important to understand that the housing provider may not refuse a request for reasonable accommodations or modifications unless it can prove that the request would impose an **undue hardship**. The provider also cannot require that tenants pay for accommodations related to disability unless the accommodations are specific to the tenant's needs and the cost is disproportionate.

Special Laws Related to Disability in Housing

In addition to reasonable accommodations and modifications, there are several unique circumstances under the FHA and other laws that specifically address disability-related issues in housing:

1. **Assistance Animals (Service and Emotional Support Animals)**
   Assistance animals, which include both service animals and emotional support animals, are not considered "pets" under the FHA.

- **Service Animals:** Trained to perform tasks for individuals with disabilities, such as guiding a blind tenant or alerting a deaf tenant.

- **Emotional Support Animals:** Provide therapeutic benefits for individuals with mental health disabilities, such as depression or PTSD. Housing providers must allow assistance animals regardless of pet policies and cannot charge pet fees or deposits, though they may charge for damages caused by the animal.

2. **Live-In Aides**

   Individuals with disabilities may need live-in aides to provide personal care or assistance. Housing providers must allow a live-in aide as a reasonable accommodation, even if the building has occupancy limits or restrictions on unrelated occupants.

3. **Reserved Parking Spaces**

   Tenants with mobility impairments may request reserved parking spaces as a reasonable accommodation, even if parking spaces are generally unassigned or require an additional fee.

4. **Accessibility in New Construction**

   Multi-family housing built after March 13, 1991, must comply with accessibility standards, including:

   - Wider doorways for wheelchair access.
   - Accessible routes through the unit and building.
   - Reinforced bathroom walls to support grab bars.

5. **Relocation Assistance in Federally Funded Housing**

   If a federally funded housing provider cannot make a unit accessible, they may be required to assist the tenant in relocating to an accessible unit, including covering associated costs.

6. **Privacy and Confidentiality of Disability Information**

   Housing providers can only ask about the nature or extent of a tenant's disability if the tenant requests an accommodation or modification. This information must be kept confidential and only used to evaluate the request.

7. **Harassment Protections**

   Tenants with disabilities are protected against harassment by landlords, staff, or other tenants. Landlords must take steps to address complaints of disability-based harassment, such as mocking or excluding tenants due to their disability.

8. **Flexible Policies for Disability-Related Income**

   Housing providers must accommodate tenants who rely on disability-related income, such as Social Security Disability Insurance (SSDI). For example, a landlord may need to offer a rent payment extension if the tenant's disability benefits are delayed.

9. **Exceptions to Zoning Laws for Group Homes**

   Zoning laws cannot impose discriminatory restrictions on group homes for individuals with disabilities. For example, group homes must be permitted in residential neighborhoods, and unreasonable distance requirements or occupancy limits may be challenged as discriminatory.

10. **Protections Against Retaliation**

    Retaliation against tenants who assert their disability rights is prohibited. Examples include raising rent, refusing to renew a lease, or threatening eviction in response to a tenant requesting accommodations.

11. **Breaking a Lease Early Due to Disability**

    While general landlord-tenant laws govern most lease agreements, tenants with disabilities may have unique rights under federal and state laws, particularly if their disability significantly affects their ability to live in their current housing. These situations often involve a legal concept called **constructive eviction** or exceptions based on reasonable accommodations under the FHA.

Tenants with disabilities may need to terminate their lease early due to a significant change in their health or living circumstances.

Key Scenarios Where Disability May Allow Lease Termination

1. **Failure to Provide Reasonable Accommodations or Modifications**

   If a landlord refuses to make reasonable accommodations or modifications that are necessary for the tenant to use and enjoy the rental property, the tenant may have grounds to terminate the lease. For example:

   - A tenant with mobility issues requests a ramp installation to access their apartment, but the landlord refuses without valid justification.
   - A landlord denies a tenant's request for an emotional support animal despite proper documentation.

Legal Basis: The tenant could argue that the refusal to accommodate constitutes a breach of the lease or a violation of the FHA, which may allow lease termination without penalties.

2. **Health and Safety Concerns Related to the Disability**

   If a tenant's housing conditions worsen their disability or jeopardize their health, they may be able to break the lease. Examples include:

   - An apartment with excessive mold, triggering severe asthma or respiratory issues.
   - Housing in a noisy environment that exacerbates a tenant's sensory sensitivities due to autism.

Legal Basis: These conditions may render the property uninhabitable, justifying lease termination under local housing laws or through constructive eviction claims.

3. **Relocation to an Accessible Facility**

If a tenant with a disability needs to move to a more accessible home or facility (e.g., an assisted living community), some state laws or reasonable accommodations under the FHA may allow them to break the lease without penalties.

Legal Basis: While not explicitly covered by the FHA, tenants can request reasonable accommodations from landlords to terminate the lease due to the disability-related need to relocate.

---

4. **Domestic Violence or Harassment Related to Disability**

    If a tenant faces harassment or violence in their current housing related to their disability, they may have the right to terminate the lease under state housing laws or the FHA. Examples include:

    - A landlord or neighbor consistently harasses the tenant about their disability.
    - The tenant experiences stalking or domestic violence that exacerbates a disability.

Legal Basis: Many states have specific statutes allowing victims of harassment or domestic violence to break their lease early.

How to Break a Lease Under Disability-Related Circumstances

If you believe your situation qualifies for early lease termination due to a disability-related issue, follow these steps:

1. **Document the Issue**
    - Keep records of any requests for accommodations, correspondence with your landlord, and evidence of how the housing affects your disability.

2. **Request a Reasonable Accommodation**

- Before attempting to break the lease, formally request accommodations from your landlord, such as modifications, repairs, or an early termination agreement.

3. **Provide Medical or Legal Documentation**
   - If applicable, submit documentation from a medical professional explaining why the current housing situation is unsuitable or inaccessible due to your disability.

4. **Consult Local Laws**
   - Check state and local landlord-tenant laws for additional protections that may apply to your situation.

5. **Seek Legal Assistance**
   - If the landlord refuses your requests, consult a fair housing attorney to explore your options under the FHA or ADA.

Alternative Solutions

If lease termination is not immediately possible or practical, the following alternatives may help:

- **Subletting or Transferring the Lease:** With the landlord's approval, you may be able to find another tenant to take over your lease.

- **Mediation or Negotiation:** A housing mediator or legal advocate can assist in negotiating lease termination terms with the landlord.

- **Filing a Complaint with HUD:** If discrimination is involved, file a complaint with the U.S. Department of Housing and Urban Development (HUD).

Conclusion

Breaking a lease due to disability is a complex process but may be justified under certain conditions, especially if the landlord fails to meet their legal obligations under the FHA. By understanding your rights and following proper procedures, you can protect yourself from penalties and discrimination while securing housing that meets your needs.

Dealing with Housing Discrimination

Housing discrimination is a serious issue that can have a significant impact on an individual's ability to live independently and enjoy the benefits of housing. Discrimination can occur in several ways, often taking place during the application process or in terms of access to accommodations or services. Common examples of housing discrimination based on disability include:

1. **Denial of Housing**: If a landlord refuses to rent or sell a home to someone with a disability, this is a clear violation of the Fair Housing Act. For instance, a landlord cannot tell a prospective tenant that they do not rent to individuals with physical disabilities or mental health conditions.

2. **Unreasonable Refusals for Modifications or Accommodations**: Discrimination can occur if a housing provider refuses a tenant's request for a reasonable modification or accommodation without providing a valid reason. For example, a tenant requesting a ramp for their wheelchair might be denied, even though such a modification would not create an undue burden on the property owner.

3. **Different Treatment in the Application Process**: If you are asked to provide additional, unnecessary information or documentation about your disability during the housing application process, this could be discrimination. A landlord cannot ask intrusive questions about the nature of your disability or require unnecessary medical records beyond what is needed to verify the accommodation request.

4. **Refusal to Allow Assistance Animals**: Under the FHA, landlords must allow individuals with disabilities to live with their service animals or emotional support animals, even in buildings with no-pet policies. Denying a request for a service

animal can be discriminatory, as service animals are considered essential for many individuals with disabilities.

5. **Unequal Terms or Conditions**: Housing providers cannot set terms or conditions for tenants with disabilities that are different from those for other tenants. For example, if a person with a disability is charged a higher security deposit than other tenants due to their disability, this constitutes discrimination.

6. **Harassment**: Discrimination can also take the form of harassment. Harassment might include comments or actions that make it difficult for someone with a disability to enjoy their home. For instance, if a landlord or another tenant makes derogatory remarks or creates a hostile living environment based on the tenant's disability, it may be considered discriminatory.

What to Do If Discrimination Occurs

If you believe you've been a victim of housing discrimination, there are several actions you can take to protect your rights:

1. **Document the Incident**: The first step in addressing housing discrimination is to keep thorough records of the incident. Note the date, time, location, the people involved, and any conversations or interactions that might be relevant. Keep copies of any written communication, such as emails, letters, or notices, that could support your claim.

2. **Try to Resolve the Issue Informally**: If possible, attempt to resolve the issue directly with the housing provider. It may be helpful to explain your rights under the Fair Housing Act and make a formal request for accommodations or modifications. Sometimes, a polite conversation can lead to a resolution without needing further escalation.

3. **File a Complaint with HUD**: If the issue cannot be resolved informally, you can file a formal complaint with the **U.S. Department of Housing and Urban Development (HUD)**. HUD is responsible for enforcing the Fair Housing Act and will investigate complaints of housing discrimination. Complaints must be filed within one year of the alleged discriminatory act.

4. **Contact Local Fair Housing Agencies**: Many states and municipalities have local agencies that investigate housing discrimination claims. These agencies can provide valuable resources and help guide you through the complaint process. In some cases, they may also offer mediation services to help resolve disputes.

5. **Seek Legal Counsel**: If you are unable to resolve the issue through HUD or local agencies, or if you wish to pursue legal action, it may be beneficial to consult with an attorney who specializes in fair housing law. An attorney can help you understand your options and represent you in court if necessary.

Examples of Disability Discrimination in Housing

Refusal to Rent Due to Mobility Impairment

James, who uses a wheelchair, finds an apartment that meets his needs, but the landlord refuses to rent to him when he discloses his mobility impairment. The apartment complex has a set of stairs at the entrance, and the landlord argues that the complex was "not designed for someone like you" and that "ramps would be a hassle." James requests a reasonable accommodation in the form of a ramp or an alternative accessible entrance, but the landlord refuses to consider any changes to the property and tells James to look elsewhere.

Discrimination Type: Refusal to rent based on disability.

Violation: Under the Fair Housing Act (FHA), landlords cannot discriminate against individuals with disabilities, and must make reasonable accommodations to ensure they have equal access to housing.

Unnecessary Additional Fees for Service Animals

Lena, who is visually impaired, applies to rent an apartment and requests permission to live with her guide dog. The landlord initially agrees but imposes a non-refundable pet fee of $500, even though the FHA explicitly states that service animals should not be subject to such fees. When Lena questions this charge, the landlord insists, "That's the policy for all pets, and you'll need to pay it." Lena believes this to be discriminatory, as the FHA requires that landlords make reasonable accommodations for service animals without charging additional fees.

Discrimination Type: Charging unnecessary fees for a service animal.
Violation: The FHA prohibits landlords from charging pet fees for service animals or emotional support animals, which are not considered pets under the law.

Inaccessible Parking Space

Maria, who uses a wheelchair, moves into a newly built apartment complex. The building is supposed to have designated accessible parking spaces, but after a few weeks of living there, Maria notices that these spaces are often taken by tenants without disabilities. She requests a reserved accessible parking space near her unit, but the property manager dismisses her request, claiming that "there is no extra space available" and suggesting that she "park further away and walk to her apartment." Maria is frustrated by the lack of attention to her needs, as other residents with disabilities are also having difficulty accessing their parking spaces.

Discrimination Type: Denial of a reasonable accommodation (parking space).

Violation: The FHA requires that landlords provide accessible parking spaces for tenants with disabilities. When those spaces are not available or are blocked, reasonable accommodations should be made, such as guaranteeing a designated accessible spot.

Harassment by Neighbors Due to Mental Health Condition

Anna, who has bipolar disorder, is living in a townhouse community. After her neighbors learn about her condition, they begin making demeaning comments, calling her "unstable," "crazy," and "dangerous." Anna's neighbor, who lives next door, frequently asks her questions about her treatment, which she finds intrusive and offensive. When Anna reports the harassment to the landlord, they brush it off, stating, "It's just concern from the neighbors; they don't mean harm." The landlord fails to address the harassment and does nothing to ensure Anna's right to live in a peaceful, respectful environment.

Discrimination Type: Harassment due to mental health disability.

Violation: Harassment due to a disability is a violation of the FHA, which requires landlords to take reasonable steps to stop discrimination and create an inclusive, supportive living environment.

Denial of Request for Modifications (Grab Bars)

Carlos, who has limited mobility after an accident, moves into a new apartment. He requests to install grab bars in the bathroom to assist with his safety while using the shower. The landlord refuses, claiming that installing grab bars would "damage the walls" and that it would be too costly. Carlos offers to cover the cost of installation himself and remove the grab bars when he moves out, but the landlord still refuses, stating that the building management has a strict policy against modifications.

Discrimination Type: Denial of a reasonable modification.

Violation: The FHA requires that landlords allow tenants with disabilities to make modifications to their units at their own expense if it is necessary for their use and enjoyment of the dwelling.

Discriminatory Terms in Lease Agreement

Evelyn, who uses a prosthetic leg, applies for a rental apartment. The landlord, upon learning of her disability, demands that she pay a higher security deposit, stating, "You might cause more damage than other tenants." The landlord imposes this condition solely because of Evelyn's disability, despite her spotless rental history. Other tenants are not asked to pay higher deposits. Evelyn challenges the unfair treatment, but the landlord insists that "the policy is there for a reason."

Discrimination Type: Differential treatment based on disability in lease terms.

Violation: The FHA prohibits landlords from requiring higher security deposits or additional fees for tenants with disabilities unless such terms are applied to all tenants.

Eviction Due to Disability-Related Behavior

Steven, a tenant with autism, occasionally exhibits repetitive vocalizations and pacing due to his condition. His neighbors complain that his behavior is disturbing the peace, even though Steven's behavior does not interfere with others. When the landlord receives complaints, they issue Steven an eviction notice, claiming that his behavior "disrupts the community" despite no prior warnings. Steven requests a reasonable accommodation in the form of a quiet corner unit or soundproofing, but the landlord dismisses his request, stating that the complex cannot accommodate his behavior.

Discrimination Type: Eviction due to disability-related behavior.

Violation: Under the FHA, evicting a tenant for behaviors related to a disability is discriminatory unless the behavior constitutes a direct threat to the health or safety of others, which must be supported by objective evidence.

Refusal to Modify Pet Policy for Emotional Support Animal

Jennifer, who has anxiety and depression, requests permission to keep her emotional support animal in an apartment that has a no-pets policy. The landlord denies the request, stating that emotional support animals "don't count as real service animals" and cannot be allowed in the unit. Despite providing documentation from her healthcare provider, the landlord refuses to make an accommodation.

Discrimination Type: Denial of reasonable accommodation for an emotional support animal.

Violation: The FHA mandates that landlords make reasonable accommodations for individuals with disabilities to keep emotional support animals, even in properties with a no-pets policy.

Inaccessible Common Areas

Michael, who uses a wheelchair, moves into a new apartment building with shared amenities such as a garden and a fitness center. He quickly discovers that the garden is only accessible via a set of stairs, and the gym has no accessible equipment or pathways. When Michael requests that the landlord install a ramp to the garden or make modifications to the gym for wheelchair access, the landlord refuses, saying that the complex was "designed as is."

Discrimination Type: Denial of access to public/common areas due to disability.
Violation: Under the FHA, landlords are required to make public or common areas accessible to tenants with disabilities. This includes ensuring that amenities like gardens and fitness centers are usable by all residents.

Unfair Application Process Due to Disability

Lucy, who has a mental health disability, applies for an apartment. During her interview, the landlord asks intrusive questions about her disability, such as whether she has been hospitalized for mental health treatment or if she has ever been in therapy. The landlord then denies her application, stating, "We're concerned about your ability to handle the responsibilities of the apartment." However, Lucy meets all other qualifications and has never been late with rent in her previous tenancies.

Discrimination Type: Discriminatory questioning and rejection based on disability.
Violation: The FHA prohibits landlords from inquiring about a prospective tenant's disability status in a way that would discourage them from applying, and it bars discrimination based on mental health or any other disability.

These expanded scenarios illustrate the many forms of disability discrimination in housing, from the denial of accommodations and modifications to harassment and unfair lease terms. The FHA and other housing laws work to ensure that individuals with disabilities have equal access to housing opportunities, protections against discrimination, and the ability to request reasonable accommodations or modifications to make their living spaces accessible.

Conclusion

Understanding your housing rights is critical to ensuring that you can access housing without discrimination. The **Fair Housing Act** provides essential protections for individuals with disabilities, ensuring that they have equal access to housing, reasonable accommodations, and modifications. Recognizing the signs of discrimination and knowing how to address issues through documentation, complaints, and legal action is key to preserving your right to live independently in a home that meets your needs. By asserting your rights and seeking help when necessary, you can protect yourself from housing discrimination and enjoy the same opportunities for housing that everyone deserves.

Chapter 7: Healthcare Rights and Medical Advocacy

Equal Access to Healthcare

Under the Americans with Disabilities Act (ADA) and Section 504 of the Rehabilitation Act, individuals with disabilities are guaranteed the right to access healthcare services on an equal basis with individuals without disabilities. These laws require healthcare providers to take appropriate steps to ensure that patients with disabilities are not excluded, segregated, or treated differently from other patients. This includes ensuring that healthcare facilities are physically accessible and that necessary modifications are made to accommodate individuals with disabilities.

Healthcare providers are also required to provide effective communication for individuals with hearing, vision, or speech disabilities. This may involve offering sign language interpreters, providing materials in alternative formats (like braille or large print), or using speech-to-text technology to ensure that communication is clear.

For instance, a hospital must have accessible examination rooms and equipment, such as adjustable-height examination tables, for individuals who use wheelchairs or have other mobility impairments. Likewise, a healthcare provider should make reasonable modifications to their policies to accommodate patients with disabilities, such as allowing extra time for appointments if needed or ensuring that the patient's specific needs are taken into account when discussing treatment plans.

Example: A wheelchair user goes to a doctor's office for a routine check-up. The building has an accessible entrance, but the examination table is too high to allow the patient to transfer from their wheelchair to the table independently. The office staff is required by law to provide an accessible table or assist the patient in transferring to the standard examination table.

Disability-Specific Services

Disability-specific services are medical treatments, support, and accommodations designed to address the unique needs of individuals with disabilities. These services may range from specialized therapies for individuals with cognitive disabilities to the provision of accessible medical equipment for those with mobility or sensory impairments.

People with intellectual or developmental disabilities may require additional time to complete medical procedures, and healthcare providers may need to adapt their communication style or approach to ensure the patient understands the information being provided. Additionally, some medical conditions, such as cerebral palsy or multiple sclerosis, may require specialized medical treatments or equipment that address specific physical needs.

For individuals with sensory disabilities, healthcare providers must ensure that there is adequate support for communication, such as providing sign language interpreters for deaf patients, or ensuring that appointments are scheduled at times when support services like interpreters are available.

Example: A patient with hearing loss needs a medical consultation for a heart condition. The doctor must arrange for a sign language interpreter or provide written materials explaining the diagnosis and treatment options in a format accessible to the patient, such as through captioned video or text-based communication.

Special Laws in Healthcare for Individuals with Disabilities

There are several disability-related special circumstances in healthcare. These circumstances are designed to ensure individuals with disabilities receive equitable access to medical services, facilities, and care under laws such as the **Americans with Disabilities Act (ADA), Section 504 of the Rehabilitation Act**, and the **Affordable Care Act (ACA)**. Below are key areas and examples:

1. Physical Accessibility of Healthcare Facilities

Healthcare facilities must provide physical access to individuals with mobility impairments. This includes:

- Accessible entrances, parking spaces, and ramps.
- Adjustable examination tables and chairs to accommodate wheelchairs.

- Lifts or hoists for transferring patients with limited mobility.
- Accessible restrooms and waiting areas.

2. Effective Communication for Patients with Disabilities

Healthcare providers must ensure effective communication with patients who have disabilities. This includes:

- Providing sign language interpreters for patients who are deaf or hard of hearing.
- Offering written materials in accessible formats, such as large print, Braille, or electronic formats for patients with visual impairments.
- Using communication boards or assistive technology for patients with speech impairments.
- Ensuring all medical instructions and diagnoses are communicated clearly and effectively.

3. Reasonable Accommodations

Healthcare providers must make reasonable accommodations to ensure patients with disabilities can access care, including:

- Scheduling extra time for appointments to address complex needs.
- Allowing service animals in examination rooms.
- Modifying policies, such as permitting a caregiver or companion to be present during medical procedures for individuals who need assistance with communication or mobility.

4. Disability-Specific Healthcare Needs

Providers must accommodate disability-related needs, such as:

- Ensuring that diagnostic equipment (e.g., mammography machines) is accessible to individuals with mobility impairments.
- Providing sensory-friendly environments for patients with autism or sensory processing disorders.

- Offering mental health support tailored to individuals with intellectual or developmental disabilities.

5. Nondiscrimination in Medical Treatment

It is illegal to deny care or provide substandard care based on a patient's disability. Examples include:

- Ensuring that individuals with disabilities are not deprioritized for organ transplants or life-saving treatments.
- Treating all patients equitably, regardless of their physical or mental condition.

6. Training for Healthcare Providers

Healthcare professionals must be trained to understand and respect the rights and needs of individuals with disabilities, including:

- Recognizing implicit biases that could affect treatment decisions.
- Learning how to assist patients with mobility devices or sensory impairments.

7. Accessible Emergency Services

Hospitals and emergency services must provide accessibility during emergencies, such as:

- Ensuring that emergency rooms are equipped to accommodate mobility devices.
- Offering interpreters or communication aids for patients during urgent care.

8. Insurance Coverage and Nondiscrimination

Under the ACA and other laws, insurance providers cannot discriminate against individuals with disabilities by:

- Denying coverage for pre-existing conditions related to a disability.
- Excluding disability-specific treatments or medications from coverage.
- Setting higher premiums or copays for individuals with disabilities.

9. Home Healthcare and Durable Medical Equipment (DME)

Healthcare providers must accommodate patients who require home healthcare or DME, such as:

- Delivering care in patients' homes for those unable to travel.
- Providing and maintaining equipment like wheelchairs, oxygen tanks, and home hospital beds.

10. Emergency Preparedness and Accessibility

Hospitals and healthcare providers must account for patients with disabilities in their emergency preparedness plans, such as:

- Ensuring that evacuation procedures include accessible routes and assistance for individuals with mobility impairments.
- Maintaining backup communication methods for individuals with hearing or speech disabilities during power outages.

11. Reproductive Healthcare

Healthcare providers must ensure that reproductive services are accessible to individuals with disabilities, including:

- Accessible examination equipment for gynecological care.
- Clear communication about family planning and pregnancy options.

12. Mental Health Services

Mental health services must be tailored to accommodate individuals with disabilities, such as:

- Offering therapy sessions in accessible formats, including telehealth for patients who cannot travel.
- Providing specialized mental health services for individuals with intellectual or developmental disabilities.

13. Special Considerations for Long-Term Care Facilities

Nursing homes and assisted living facilities must ensure accessibility, including:

- Providing accessible rooms, bathrooms, and common areas.
- Allowing residents to maintain autonomy and access to personal mobility devices or assistive technology.

14. Service Animal Access

Healthcare providers must allow service animals to accompany patients into treatment areas unless the presence of the animal compromises the sterile field or patient safety.

15. Preventing Discriminatory Practices

Healthcare providers cannot:

- Refuse to accept new patients with disabilities.
- Require unnecessary medical documentation to provide accommodations.
- Assume that patients with disabilities have a lower quality of life or reduced ability to make medical decisions.

16. Accessible Telehealth Services

With the growing use of telehealth, providers must ensure that virtual healthcare platforms are accessible to individuals with disabilities by:

- Providing captioning or sign language interpreters during virtual consultations.
- Ensuring platforms are compatible with screen readers or other assistive technology.

17. Advocacy and Complaint Mechanisms

Patients with disabilities who face discrimination or lack of accessibility in healthcare can file complaints with:

- The Office for Civil Rights (OCR) under the U.S. Department of Health and Human Services (HHS).
- State or local disability advocacy organizations.

By addressing these special circumstances, healthcare systems can ensure that individuals with disabilities receive equitable and respectful care tailored to their needs.

Advocating for Yourself in Healthcare Settings

Communicating Your Needs

One of the most important steps in advocating for your rights in healthcare settings is to ensure that your needs are communicated effectively to your healthcare provider. Clear communication is essential to receiving the accommodations and services you need.

To ensure your healthcare provider understands your needs:

- **Know Your Rights**: Familiarize yourself with the ADA and Section 504 protections to ensure that you know what accommodations you are entitled to request.

- **Be Specific**: When you are requesting an accommodation, provide details about your disability and what adjustments are necessary for you to receive effective healthcare. For example, if you need extra time during your appointment due to a cognitive disability, ask for this in advance when scheduling your appointment.

- **Use Assistive Devices**: If you need assistive devices or accommodations, make sure to bring them with you to your appointments. This can include hearing aids, mobility aids, or any other tools that help you communicate effectively or access healthcare.

- **Request Support**: If you need help navigating the healthcare system or advocating for your rights, consider bringing a family member, friend, or advocate to your appointment. They can help ensure that you are receiving the accommodations you need and can assist with communication if needed.

Example: If you have a cognitive disability that impacts your ability to understand complex medical terms, you might ask the healthcare provider to explain things more slowly or use simpler language. You could also request written materials that explain your diagnosis in clear, simple language.

Challenges in Healthcare

Despite the laws and regulations that protect individuals with disabilities, many people still face significant challenges when seeking medical care. Some of these challenges are structural and systemic, while others may arise from unconscious bias or ignorance by healthcare providers.

- **Substandard Care**: Discriminatory attitudes or lack of knowledge about a particular disability may lead healthcare providers to offer substandard care. For example, a healthcare provider might assume that a patient with a disability does not need the same level of care as other patients or fail to recognize that a disability can impact a patient's overall health in complex ways.

- **Neglect and Ignorance**: In some cases, healthcare professionals may overlook or dismiss the needs of patients with disabilities. This could manifest as neglect during a hospital stay, where a nurse or doctor fails to provide necessary accommodations like positioning assistance or extra time to understand treatment options.

- **Inaccessible Medical Equipment**: Many hospitals and medical offices are not equipped with specialized tools that are necessary for individuals with disabilities. For example, an MRI machine that is too narrow for someone who uses a wheelchair, or medical examination tables that are not adjustable, can create barriers to receiving adequate healthcare.

Example: A person with multiple sclerosis visits a clinic for a routine check-up, but the office does not have an accessible bathroom or equipment that accommodates her mobility needs. As a result, she cannot complete certain diagnostic tests and must leave the clinic without receiving the necessary care.

Resolving Healthcare Barriers

Legal Recourse

If you face discrimination or are unable to access healthcare services due to your disability, there are several legal recourses available:

- **File a Complaint with the Office for Civil Rights (OCR):** If a healthcare provider or facility is violating the rights of individuals with disabilities, you can file a complaint with the OCR at the U.S. Department of Health and Human Services (HHS). The OCR investigates complaints of discrimination and ensures compliance with Section 504 of the Rehabilitation Act and the ADA.

- **File a Complaint with State or Local Agencies:** Many states have agencies that handle complaints of discrimination in healthcare. These agencies can help mediate disputes or investigate complaints of healthcare discrimination.

- **Legal Action:** If your case is not resolved through complaints or other avenues, you may have the option of filing a lawsuit in court. In some cases, you can seek legal counsel to assist with filing a lawsuit against healthcare providers, hospitals, or other medical institutions for disability discrimination.

Example: If a person with a visual impairment is denied access to written materials in an accessible format, they may file a complaint with the OCR. If the issue persists, they could take legal action to ensure that the healthcare facility complies with the ADA.

Support Organizations

Many organizations are dedicated to assisting individuals with disabilities in navigating healthcare systems and advocating for their rights. These organizations provide support, resources, and advocacy services for people facing discrimination or barriers in healthcare.

- **National Disability Rights Network (NDRN):** This organization provides legal advocacy and protection for individuals with disabilities, helping them fight discrimination and ensuring equal access to healthcare and other services.

- **American Disabilities Act National Network (ADA National Network):** The ADA National Network offers resources and training for individuals with disabilities to understand their rights and advocate for themselves in healthcare settings.

- **Specific Disability-Related Advocacy Groups:** For individuals with specific disabilities, there are national and local advocacy groups that specialize in healthcare access. For example, the American Foundation for the Blind or the

National Association of the Deaf can provide assistance and guidance for individuals with visual or hearing impairments.

Example: The National Association of the Deaf (NAD) can assist a deaf patient in ensuring that their healthcare provider provides an interpreter for appointments or that all communications are accessible, including medical information and follow-up instructions.

Examples of Disability Discrimination in Healthcare

Denied Access to Treatment (Mobility Impairment)

Scenario:
Sarah, who uses a wheelchair due to a spinal cord injury, arrives at her local hospital for a routine check-up. When she checks in, the receptionist informs her that the examination room assigned to her is not wheelchair accessible, as it is located on the second floor and there is no elevator. Sarah requests to be moved to a more accessible room, but the staff tells her that no accommodations can be made because the building is an older facility. The receptionist offers no alternative arrangements, and Sarah is told to either reschedule her appointment or visit another healthcare provider, despite her condition being urgent.

Discrimination:
This situation exemplifies the denial of equal access to healthcare services. Under the Americans with Disabilities Act (ADA), healthcare providers are required to make their facilities accessible to individuals with mobility impairments, including offering accessible examination rooms and making reasonable accommodations for people with disabilities.

Failure to Provide Communication Access (Deaf/Hearing Impaired)

Scenario:
Mark, who is deaf, has an appointment with his primary care physician. Upon arrival, Mark requests a sign language interpreter, as he has difficulty understanding the physician without one. The receptionist informs him that the clinic does not typically offer sign

language interpreters because of cost concerns. Mark tries to communicate through written notes, but the doctor, who is not accustomed to working with deaf patients, struggles to understand and becomes visibly frustrated. Mark leaves the appointment without clear communication about his medical concerns.

Discrimination:

This situation represents a failure to provide effective communication, which is a violation of the ADA. Healthcare providers are required to ensure that patients with hearing impairments have access to the services they need, which can include providing qualified interpreters or other means of communication.

Ignoring Medical Needs (Intellectual Disability)

Scenario:

Carla, who has an intellectual disability, visits an emergency room after she is involved in a minor car accident. While waiting to be seen, Carla repeatedly informs the staff that she is experiencing pain, but they dismiss her complaints, attributing her behavior to her disability. When she is finally seen by a physician, he assumes that she does not understand the severity of her injuries and orders only minimal tests, despite her ongoing pain. The doctor discharges Carla without further investigation, assuming she will recover without complication.

Discrimination:

This scenario shows how assumptions about an individual's intellectual disability can lead to inadequate medical care. Healthcare providers are obligated to provide appropriate care regardless of intellectual disabilities, and patients should not be dismissed based on their ability to communicate or understand complex medical information.

Inaccessible Medical Equipment (Visual Impairment)

Scenario:

Jason, who is blind, goes to a clinic for a routine eye exam, though he does not need vision correction. Upon arrival, the nurse asks him to fill out forms about his medical history, but the forms are only available in print format. Jason requests a version in braille or an accessible digital format but is told that the clinic doesn't provide them. The nurse offers no alternative accommodations, leaving Jason unable to complete the necessary paperwork. Eventually, Jason is told to reschedule his appointment for a time when accessible forms can be provided.

Discrimination:

This is an example of failure to provide accommodations for patients with visual impairments. The clinic's refusal to provide accessible forms violates the rights of individuals with disabilities under the ADA and limits their access to care.

Refusal to Prescribe Medication (Mental Health Disability)

Scenario:

Linda, who has been diagnosed with bipolar disorder, visits her psychiatrist for a follow-up. During the appointment, she requests a specific medication that has worked well for her in the past. However, her doctor refuses to prescribe it, stating that people with mental health conditions should not be prescribed such medications due to potential misuse or abuse. The psychiatrist suggests that Linda should rely on "less potent" alternatives and dismisses her concerns about the effectiveness of these treatments.

Discrimination:

This case demonstrates discriminatory treatment based on mental health disability. Medical professionals should not refuse treatment or medications simply because a patient has a mental health condition. Such refusals violate the patient's right to appropriate medical care and the autonomy of individuals to make informed choices about their treatment.

Inaccessible Doctor's Office (Mobility Impairment)

Scenario:

Alex, who uses a scooter due to limited mobility from a neurological condition, arrives at his primary care provider's office. Upon arrival, he finds that the front door is too narrow to accommodate his scooter, and there are no accessible parking spaces nearby. When Alex alerts the receptionist to the accessibility issues, they simply tell him to come back with a different mode of transportation. Alex is not offered any alternative options or referrals to other healthcare providers who might be more accommodating.

Discrimination:

This situation reflects a failure to provide physical access to healthcare services. The medical office is required by law to make its facilities accessible to individuals with mobility impairments, including offering accessible entrances and parking spaces, under the ADA.

Lack of Disability Awareness (Cognitive Disability)

Scenario:

Emily, who has autism, goes for a routine check-up at her healthcare provider's office. During the appointment, Emily struggles with eye contact and has difficulty processing verbal instructions, so she speaks in a slightly disjointed manner. The physician assumes she is uninterested or uncooperative and becomes visibly frustrated. Rather than adjusting the communication method or taking extra time to accommodate Emily's needs, the doctor ends the appointment early, suggesting that Emily might not be a good candidate for the required medical treatment.

Discrimination:

This case illustrates the discrimination that can occur when healthcare providers fail to understand the specific communication needs of patients with cognitive disabilities. Providers are required to make reasonable adjustments, such as taking extra time or using alternative communication methods, to ensure that all patients receive the care they need.

Failure to Recognize the Need for Assistive Devices (Hearing Impairment)

Scenario:

Patricia, who is profoundly deaf, attends an appointment at a clinic for an annual check-up. She requests a sign language interpreter, but the clinic staff informs her that they don't offer such services. Patricia is told she can rely on lip-reading, but the physician is not accustomed to communicating through lip-reading and does not make any effort to ensure Patricia understands the medical instructions. As a result, Patricia leaves the appointment with little understanding of her health status.

Discrimination:

This situation highlights the failure to provide effective communication services to individuals who are deaf or hard of hearing. Under the ADA, healthcare providers are required to make reasonable accommodations, such as offering interpreters or other communication support.

Rushed Consultation Without Consideration for Disability (Chronic Pain)

Scenario:

Jack, who suffers from chronic pain due to fibromyalgia, attends a scheduled consultation with a pain specialist. When he explains his condition and asks for more time during the appointment to discuss potential treatment options, the doctor refuses, stating that the appointment is only 15 minutes long and should be enough for a "simple" consultation. Jack's pain management needs are complex, but the doctor insists on a quick appointment, leaving Jack with limited options for managing his condition.

Discrimination:

This case illustrates how individuals with chronic pain conditions can be treated dismissively by healthcare professionals. People with chronic conditions often require more time to discuss treatment plans, and it is discriminatory for healthcare providers to rush consultations or dismiss a patient's needs.

Refusal of Service (Physical Disability)

Scenario:

Mia, a woman with cerebral palsy, contacts a specialist's office for an appointment regarding her condition. The receptionist tells Mia that the clinic cannot accommodate her because their offices are not wheelchair accessible and that they do not have the resources to assist individuals with mobility impairments. No effort is made to provide alternative solutions, such as a referral to a more accessible clinic or arranging accommodations for Mia.

Discrimination:

This scenario demonstrates outright refusal of service based on disability, a clear violation of ADA protections. Healthcare providers must not refuse to treat individuals with disabilities simply because they may require accommodations.

These hypotheticals provide a broad range of scenarios that exemplify the different ways disability discrimination can manifest in healthcare settings. From inaccessibility and failure to accommodate communication needs to assumptions based on a patient's disability, each scenario underscores the importance of creating an inclusive and accessible healthcare system for everyone, regardless of their disabilities.

Conclusion

Your right to access healthcare services, receive reasonable accommodations, and be treated without discrimination is guaranteed by law. While navigating the healthcare system can be challenging, understanding your rights and knowing how to advocate for yourself can ensure you receive the care you need. If you encounter barriers to care, there are numerous resources available to help you resolve issues, including filing complaints, seeking legal assistance, and connecting with advocacy organizations. By advocating for yourself and working to remove barriers, you can ensure that your healthcare needs are met with dignity, respect, and fairness.

Chapter 8: Transportation Rights

ADA and Transportation

The Americans with Disabilities Act (ADA) ensures that individuals with disabilities have the right to access public and private transportation services without discrimination. This legislation helps to eliminate barriers that would otherwise prevent people with disabilities from fully participating in everyday activities. These include buses, trains, and other forms of public transit, as well as taxis, rideshare services, and airlines. Understanding your rights and how to advocate for necessary accommodations when accessing transportation is crucial for those who face mobility challenges, sensory impairments, or other disabilities.

Public Transportation: Your Rights to Accessible Buses, Trains, and Other Public Transport Options

Public transportation systems—including buses, subways, trains, and light rail—must be accessible to people with disabilities. These accommodations are vital to ensuring that people with mobility, sensory, or cognitive disabilities can travel independently, confidently, and without unnecessary barriers. The ADA mandates specific design features in public transit, and transit agencies must comply with these rules to ensure equal access.

Key Rights Under the ADA:

1. **Accessible Vehicles:** Buses and trains must be equipped with features that make them accessible to individuals with mobility impairments. These may include:
    - **Wheelchair ramps** or **lifts** to enable people with disabilities to board.
    - **Reserved spaces** on buses and trains for passengers who use wheelchairs or mobility devices.
    - **Lowered platforms** at train stations for easier access to vehicles.
    - **Tie-downs** for securing mobility devices, ensuring a safe ride for all passengers.

- All of these accommodations must be available on all public buses, subways, and trains.

2. **Accessible Stations and Platforms:** Public transportation agencies must ensure that transit stations and platforms are accessible, especially for people who use wheelchairs, walkers, or other mobility aids. This includes:
    - **Ramps** and **elevators** at train stations and subway stops for access to platforms.
    - **Automatic doors** or wide manual doors for easy entry and exit.
    - **Accessible restrooms** in stations and terminals.
    - **Clear signage** in multiple formats, including tactile (Braille), audible, and visual cues, for people with sensory disabilities.

3. **Communication Assistance:** Many public transportation systems must provide accommodations for individuals with hearing or visual impairments, including:
    - **Audible announcements** of stops, train arrivals, or delays for those with visual impairments.
    - **Visual announcements** (e.g., electronic displays) showing train or bus arrival times, current stops, or delays for people with hearing impairments.
    - **Priority seating** and **audio equipment** for those who may need assistance hearing announcements.

4. **No Denial of Service:** Public transportation providers are prohibited from denying service to people with disabilities as long as they are capable of traveling independently or with the assistance of an aide. The ADA ensures that service must be provided to all individuals, regardless of the disability, and alternative transportation must be arranged if a situation arises where a vehicle cannot be fully accessible.

Private Transportation: Rights to Accommodations in Taxis, Ridesharing, and Airlines

In addition to public transportation, private transportation services, including taxis, rideshare companies, and airlines, are also required to accommodate individuals with disabilities. Ensuring that these providers comply with accessibility standards is critical for allowing people with disabilities to live fully integrated lives.

1. Taxis and Rideshare Services: Many cities and states mandate that taxi companies offer accessible vehicles. People with disabilities should be able to request a wheelchair-accessible taxi or rideshare vehicle in advance or at the time of booking.

- **Taxis:**

    Taxis must provide an accessible vehicle upon request if it is available in the area. The cab driver cannot refuse service because of your disability. They also must not charge higher fares for passengers with disabilities unless the fare is based on the actual additional time or distance required for the accommodation (e.g., extra assistance or vehicle modifications).

- **Rideshare Services (Uber, Lyft, etc.):**

    Rideshare companies are increasingly offering accessible vehicles in many areas, though availability may vary. Uber and Lyft both provide a service where riders can request accessible vehicles. If an accessible vehicle is not available, the company must make efforts to offer an alternative ride or refer you to another transportation service.

2. Air Travel: Your Rights to Accessible Air Travel

Traveling by air involves its own set of challenges for people with disabilities, but the **Air Carrier Access Act (ACAA)** offers specific protections to ensure accessibility.

Key Rights Under the ACAA:

1. **Seating Arrangements:**
    - Airlines must provide accessible seating arrangements to individuals with disabilities. This could include seats that allow for mobility aids or that are close to aisles for easy access.

- Passengers with disabilities can request specific accommodations, such as bulkhead seating (seats at the front of the aircraft), or any seating that allows for extra space and easier access to the restroom.

2. **Boarding and Deplaning Assistance:**
    - Airlines must assist individuals with disabilities during the boarding and deplaning process. This includes helping passengers onto the plane, providing boarding assistance at the gate, and aiding in transferring from a wheelchair to an airline seat if needed.
    - Special accommodations are required for passengers needing assistance during emergency evacuations.

3. **In-Flight Accommodations:**
    - During the flight, airlines are required to provide specific accommodations, including assistance with meals, accessing the restroom, or adjusting seats. For passengers who require oxygen or specific medical equipment during the flight, airlines must provide these services if requested in advance.
    - For those who are visually impaired, airlines must provide help with reading flight information or locating amenities.

4. **No Denial of Service Based on Disability:**
    - Airlines cannot refuse service to passengers with disabilities due to their disability. Airlines are required to make reasonable accommodations, such as seating arrangements and assistance, to ensure safe travel for all passengers.

Special Laws in Public and Private Transportation Services for Individuals with Disabilities

There are many disability-related special circumstances in public and private transportation services to ensure individuals with disabilities have equitable access. These provisions are mandated by the **Americans with Disabilities Act (ADA)** and other laws, ensuring that transportation systems—both public and private—are accessible and accommodating.

1. Accessible Public Transportation

Public transportation systems (e.g., buses, subways, and trains) must comply with ADA standards, which include:

- **Wheelchair-Accessible Vehicles:** Buses, trains, and other forms of public transit must have ramps, lifts, or low floors to accommodate individuals using wheelchairs or mobility devices.

- **Priority Seating:** Designated seating areas for passengers with disabilities.

- **Announcements and Signage:** Audible and visual announcements for stops, delays, and route changes to assist individuals with hearing or vision impairments.

- **Assistance Services:** Operators must assist passengers with disabilities in boarding, exiting, and securing mobility devices.

2. Paratransit Services

Paratransit is a complementary service for individuals unable to use fixed-route public transportation due to their disability. Features include:

- **Door-to-Door Service:** Personalized transportation from pick-up to destination.

- **Scheduling Assistance:** Reservations to accommodate the passenger's needs, often requiring advanced booking.

- **Comparable Fares and Service Areas:** Paratransit fares and routes must be comparable to the public transit system's fixed routes.

3. Private Transportation (Taxis, Rideshares, and Shuttles)

Private transportation providers must also accommodate individuals with disabilities:

- **Wheelchair-Accessible Taxis and Rideshares:** Companies must offer options for passengers using mobility devices, or contract with accessible vehicle services.

- **Service Animals:** Private transportation providers cannot refuse rides to individuals with service animals.

- **Driver Assistance:** Drivers must assist with loading or securing mobility devices without charging additional fees.

- **Accessible Apps and Websites:** Ride-hailing platforms like Uber and Lyft must ensure their apps are accessible to individuals with visual impairments or other disabilities.

4. Air Travel (Air Carrier Access Act - ACAA)

Airlines are required to provide specific accommodations for passengers with disabilities:

- **Pre-Boarding Assistance:** Priority boarding and staff assistance with boarding or disembarking.

- **Wheelchair Assistance:** Availability of wheelchairs for navigating the airport and boarding the aircraft.

- **Seating Accommodations:** Adjustments to ensure passengers with disabilities are seated appropriately (e.g., near exits or with companions).

- **Accessible Lavatories and In-Flight Services:** Availability of accessible bathrooms on newer aircraft and accommodations for service animals.

5. Rail Travel (Amtrak and Commuter Trains)

Rail systems must ensure accessibility for individuals with disabilities:

- **Accessible Train Cars:** Equipped with lifts or ramps for boarding, along with accessible restrooms.

- **Assistance with Boarding:** Staff must help passengers with disabilities as needed.

- **Companion Seating:** Spaces for companions to sit near passengers using wheelchairs or mobility devices.

6. Parking and Drop-Off Zones

Transportation hubs (airports, train stations, bus stops) must provide accessible parking spaces and drop-off zones for passengers with disabilities:

- **ADA-Accessible Parking:** Parking spaces close to entrances with proper signage and space for van lifts.
- **Curbside Assistance:** Help with luggage or navigating to the terminal.

7. Service Animal Access

Transportation services must allow individuals with disabilities to be accompanied by their service animals, regardless of company policies regarding pets:

- **No Additional Fees:** Passengers cannot be charged extra for traveling with a service animal.
- **Training Requirements:** Staff must be trained to interact respectfully with service animals and their owners.

8. Accessible Intercity and Long-Distance Bus Services

Providers like Greyhound must:

- **Provide Accessible Vehicles:** Ensure a percentage of their fleet is equipped to handle wheelchairs and other mobility devices.
- **Allow Reservations for Accessibility Needs:** Accommodate advance notice for accessible transportation.

9. Accessible Transportation for Emergencies

Transportation services must account for individuals with disabilities during emergencies or evacuations:

- **Accessible Evacuation Routes:** Vehicles and routes must accommodate mobility devices.
- **Communication Access:** Information about emergency changes to service must be shared in accessible formats.

10. Special Provisions for Temporary Disabilities

Individuals with temporary disabilities (e.g., recovering from surgery) may qualify for temporary accommodations, such as accessible parking permits or paratransit services.

11. Retrofitting and Future Compliance

Existing public and private transportation providers are required to make ongoing updates to improve accessibility:

- **Retrofitting Older Systems:** Older transportation systems must incorporate accessibility features when undergoing significant renovations.
- **New Construction Standards:** Newly constructed transportation hubs must fully comply with ADA requirements.

12. Complaints and Advocacy

Individuals with disabilities have the right to file complaints if they face discrimination or barriers in transportation:

- **Filing with the Department of Transportation (DOT):** Complaints regarding non-compliance with ADA or ACAA standards.
- **Local Transit Authorities:** Reporting accessibility issues for local public transit systems.

These accommodations ensure that individuals with disabilities can travel independently, safely, and with dignity in public and private transportation settings.

How to Address Transportation Barriers

Despite the strong protections provided under the ADA and ACAA, individuals with disabilities may still face barriers in accessing transportation. If you encounter challenges in obtaining accessible services or accommodations, it is important to know how to address these issues effectively.

---

1. Reporting Issues: Steps to Take If You Face Barriers in Accessing Transportation

When facing transportation barriers, it is essential to know how to report and resolve the issue. The following steps can help:

- **Document the Incident:**

    Always make a note of the time, location, individuals involved, and nature of the problem. Take photos or videos if possible. Documentation is important for filing complaints or legal action later.

- **Contact the Transportation Provider:**

    If you experience an accessibility barrier, the first step is often to contact the transportation provider directly. For example, if a bus is not accessible, you can contact the local transit authority to report the issue. Most transit agencies have an ADA coordinator who handles complaints related to accessibility. For rideshare services or airlines, contact their customer service teams or ADA compliance departments.

- **File a Complaint with Regulatory Agencies:**

    If contacting the provider does not resolve the issue, you can file a formal complaint with the appropriate regulatory agency.

    - **Public Transit:** File with the **Federal Transit Administration (FTA)** or your local transit authority's ADA office.

    - **Airlines:** File with the **Department of Transportation's Office of Aviation Enforcement and Proceedings** or the **Federal Aviation Administration (FAA)**.

    - **Taxis/Rideshare Services:** File with the **local regulatory body** or the company itself.

- **Legal Action:**

    If transportation barriers persist and are not addressed through complaints, you may pursue legal action. This could involve filing a lawsuit against the service provider for failing to comply with ADA or ACAA standards. Legal recourse can help ensure that you receive compensation and that transportation services improve for others facing similar challenges.

- **Support Organizations:**

    Several nonprofit organizations advocate for accessible transportation and can assist you with navigating barriers, including:

    - **American Association of People with Disabilities (AAPD)**
    - **National Disability Rights Network (NDRN)**
    - **Disability Rights Education & Defense Fund (DREDF)**

These organizations often provide resources, legal support, and guidance in addressing transportation challenges.

Examples of Disability Discrimination in Transportation

Denied Accessible Taxi Service

Sarah, who uses a wheelchair, schedules a taxi ride to attend an important medical appointment. When the taxi arrives, it is a regular sedan, not an accessible vehicle with a ramp or lift. Sarah tries to explain her need for an accessible vehicle, but the driver dismisses her and states that no accessible vehicles are available at the moment. He refuses to offer assistance or suggest alternative solutions. Sarah is left stranded for over an hour, missing her appointment, and the taxi service refuses to offer any form of compensation.

Discrimination: Denial of service due to disability, failure to provide accessible transportation.

Bus Ramp Failure

James, who uses a walker for mobility, attempts to board a city bus. As he approaches, the bus driver lowers the ramp, but it malfunctions and won't properly extend. The driver, instead of trying to fix it or helping James board in another way, dismisses him, saying he should wait for the next bus. James, who needs to arrive at his workplace on time, struggles to find alternative transportation, but the next bus won't arrive for another 30 minutes.

Discrimination: Failure to provide functional accessibility features, lack of assistance for passengers with mobility impairments.

Inaccessible Train Station

Emily, who is visually impaired and uses a white cane, goes to catch a train at her local station. The station lacks tactile floor markings, which would help guide her to the platform, and there are no audible signals to indicate when trains are arriving or where to board. The station staff are unaware of her presence and fail to offer assistance. Emily, feeling unsafe and unsure where to go, asks a bystander for help. After some time, she finally makes it to her train, but the experience leaves her feeling frustrated and fearful of navigating the station again.

Discrimination: Lack of accessible infrastructure and failure to provide adequate assistance to individuals with visual impairments.

Discriminatory Rideshare Driver

Mark, who is deaf, books a rideshare ride to meet a friend for dinner. When he arrives, the driver is visibly upset that Mark doesn't hear his voice and expresses frustration. Mark tries to communicate through text messages, but the driver refuses to respond to them. Instead, the driver cancels the ride, leaving Mark confused and stranded in an unfamiliar area. Mark is forced to order a second ride, but he is now late for his dinner.

Discrimination: Refusal of service and failure to accommodate communication needs, based on Mark's disability.

Airplane Seating Refusal

Maria, who has mobility challenges and requires an aisle seat for easier access to the restroom, calls ahead to request specific seating for her flight. When she boards the plane, she finds that she has been assigned a window seat instead. She approaches the flight attendant and requests to be moved to an aisle seat, but the attendant refuses, stating that all aisle seats are "unavailable" despite the fact that several aisle seats remain empty. Maria is forced to manage discomfort throughout the flight, as she has difficulty reaching the bathroom in her assigned seat.

Discrimination: Failure to provide reasonable accommodation for mobility needs during air travel.

Unwillingness to Help with Boarding

Greg, who uses a wheelchair, arrives at the airport several hours before his flight. He contacts the airline's customer service to request assistance with boarding, but when the time comes for boarding, no one shows up to help. Greg waits at the gate, visibly distressed, as the airline staff continues to ignore his requests for assistance. After missing the first boarding call, a gate agent tells him it's too late to board without help. Greg misses his flight due to the airline's lack of support and failure to meet his disability-related needs.

Discrimination: Failure to provide timely boarding assistance and support for passengers with disabilities.

Lack of Accessible Parking

Lily, who uses a scooter for mobility, arrives at a train station for her daily commute. When she tries to park in the designated accessible parking spots, she finds that all of the spaces are occupied by non-disabled drivers. She approaches station staff, who tell her that they cannot enforce accessible parking regulations. Lily, now late for work, is forced to park far from the entrance, making it difficult for her to access the platform on time.

Discrimination: Failure to provide proper accessible parking, and lack of enforcement of parking regulations.

Inaccessible Bus Stop

Tom, who uses a wheelchair, attempts to catch a bus at his regular bus stop. However, the stop is located at the top of a set of stairs, and there is no ramp or elevator to provide access for individuals with mobility challenges. When Tom signals the bus driver to stop, the driver tells him he will have to wait for the next bus, as the current bus cannot access the stop. The driver then drives away without offering further assistance. Tom is forced to wait an additional 45 minutes for the next bus, putting him at risk of missing an important work meeting.

Discrimination: Failure to ensure accessible bus stops and the inability to accommodate passengers with mobility impairments.

Refusal to Transport Service Animal

Jessica, who relies on a service dog for mobility assistance, calls a taxi service to request transportation. When the driver arrives, he refuses to let her board, claiming that his vehicle is "allergic" to animals and that no pets are allowed. Jessica tries to explain that her service dog is essential for her health and safety, but the driver refuses to budge, canceling the ride and leaving Jessica without any transportation.

Discrimination: Refusal to accommodate a service animal as required under the ADA.

Improper Assistance on a Bus

Peter, who is blind, boards a bus in the early morning to attend an important business meeting. He requests help from the bus driver to notify him when his stop approaches. The driver, annoyed by the request, tells Peter to "figure it out" and continues driving without further assistance. Peter misses his stop and is forced to take an additional 30-minute detour to reach his meeting.

Discrimination: Failure to provide adequate assistance to a visually impaired passenger, leaving them unable to navigate their route independently.

These scenarios highlight the significant barriers individuals with disabilities face in accessing transportation services. They emphasize the need for accessible infrastructure, services, and policies that cater to the diverse needs of people with disabilities.

Conclusion

Transportation is a vital aspect of daily life, and the ADA and ACAA ensure that individuals with disabilities have the right to access it without discrimination. Whether using public transit, taxis, rideshare services, or air travel, people with disabilities are entitled to reasonable accommodations and accessible services. If barriers arise, individuals can address them through complaints, legal action, or by seeking support from advocacy organizations. By understanding your rights and knowing the steps to take when transportation barriers emerge, you can help ensure that everyone has equal access to transportation and the freedom it provides.

Chapter 9: Building Confidence as an Advocate

Advocating for your rights as a person with a disability can be both empowering and daunting. Confidence doesn't always come naturally, but it can be cultivated through knowledge, preparation, and practice. In this chapter, we'll explore strategies to help you advocate effectively, handle resistance, and overcome the fear of retaliation. We'll also address ways to protect your mental and emotional health throughout the process, ensuring you remain resilient in the face of challenges.

Self-Advocacy Tips

Advocacy starts with you. Whether you're requesting accommodations, addressing accessibility barriers, or challenging discrimination, self-advocacy requires a combination of confidence, clear communication, and persistence.

Assertiveness: Confidently Asserting Your Rights

Being assertive means expressing your needs firmly and respectfully without aggression. It's about standing up for yourself while fostering constructive dialogue.

- **Understand Your Rights:** Knowledge is your foundation. Familiarize yourself with laws like the Americans with Disabilities Act (ADA), the Fair Housing Act, and any applicable state or local regulations. Knowing your rights ensures you're advocating from a position of strength.

- **Be Specific:** Clearly state what you need and why. For instance, instead of saying, "I need help," you might say, "I need access to a height-adjustable desk to perform my job effectively." Specificity leaves less room for misunderstanding or resistance.

- **Rehearse Your Request:** Practice stating your needs out loud, especially if you're nervous or expect pushback. Rehearsing with a friend or in front of a mirror can build confidence and refine your delivery.

- **Use Positive Language:** Frame your requests in terms of benefits. For example, explain how an accommodation improves productivity, ensures safety, or enhances collaboration.

- **Keep Written Records:** Document all interactions related to your advocacy, including emails, phone calls, and in-person meetings. Written evidence is invaluable if you need to escalate the issue.

Navigating Difficult Situations

Advocacy often involves engaging with individuals or organizations unfamiliar with disability rights. Challenging these barriers can lead to tense or uncomfortable situations, but the following tips can help you navigate them effectively:

- **Stay Calm and Professional:** Even if you encounter resistance or dismissiveness, maintain your composure. Take deep breaths and remain focused on the issue at hand. Responding calmly can de-escalate tension and keep the discussion productive.

- **Ask Questions:** If your request is denied or misunderstood, ask for clarification. Questions like, "Can you explain why this accommodation is not possible?" can open the door to problem-solving and expose misinformed assumptions.

- **Frame the Conversation Around Collaboration:** Position yourself as a partner in finding a solution. For example, say, "I'd like to work together to identify an adjustment that works for both of us."

- **Bring Support When Possible:** Having a trusted friend, colleague, or advocate present can provide emotional support and bolster your case. Their presence can also ensure accurate documentation of the interaction.

- **Take Breaks if Needed:** If a conversation becomes too heated or overwhelming, request a pause to regroup and revisit the discussion later. It's better to take a break than to react impulsively.

Handling Resistance

Resistance to advocacy efforts can stem from ignorance, misunderstanding, or outright prejudice. Understanding how to handle pushback is a critical skill for any advocate.

Dealing with Pushback

Resistance can manifest in various ways, such as dismissive attitudes, deflection, or outright denial of your requests. Here's how to respond effectively:

- **Remain Firm:** Politely but confidently reaffirm your needs and rights. For instance, say, "I understand your concerns, but this accommodation is essential for my participation and is protected under the ADA."

- **Focus on Education:** Resistance often stems from a lack of awareness about disability rights. Provide information or resources to help others understand the legal or practical basis for your request.

- **Involve Higher Authorities:** If you encounter persistent resistance, escalate the matter to a manager, HR representative, or regulatory body. Chain-of-command escalation ensures your concerns are addressed at the appropriate level.

- **Don't Take It Personally:** Resistance can feel like a personal rejection, but it often reflects systemic issues rather than individual animosity. Focus on the broader goal of achieving your rights.

Protecting Your Mental Health

Advocating for yourself can be emotionally draining, particularly when faced with repeated obstacles. Prioritizing your mental well-being ensures you have the resilience to continue your advocacy efforts.

- **Set Emotional Boundaries:** Decide how much energy you're willing to invest in a particular issue. It's okay to take breaks or step back if advocacy becomes overwhelming.

- **Seek a Support Network:** Connect with friends, family, or advocacy groups who can provide encouragement and share their experiences. Knowing you're not alone can alleviate feelings of isolation.

- **Engage in Self-Care:** Regularly engage in activities that relax and rejuvenate you, such as mindfulness, exercise, or creative hobbies. Taking care of yourself helps sustain your energy for advocacy.

- **Practice Gratitude:** Reflect on your progress and celebrate small wins. Recognizing your efforts, no matter how incremental, reinforces your sense of purpose and accomplishment.

Overcoming Fear of Retaliation

Fear of retaliation can deter many individuals from asserting their rights. Retaliation might include being fired, demoted, harassed, or excluded from opportunities. Fortunately, laws like the ADA and the Fair Housing Act provide robust protections against retaliation.

Legal Protections Against Retaliation

- **Understand the Law:** Retaliation is illegal under federal laws such as the ADA, the Fair Housing Act, and Title VII of the Civil Rights Act. These laws prohibit adverse actions against individuals who assert their rights or file complaints.

- **Keep Detailed Records:** Document any actions that could constitute retaliation, such as negative performance reviews following a request for accommodation or exclusion from workplace meetings after filing a complaint.

- **Act Quickly:** Report suspected retaliation to HR, a supervisor, or a regulatory agency promptly. The sooner you address the issue, the more effectively it can be resolved.

How to Address Retaliation

- **File a Formal Complaint:** If you suspect retaliation, report it to the appropriate authority. For workplace issues, this may involve filing a complaint with the Equal Employment Opportunity Commission (EEOC). For housing discrimination, contact the Department of Housing and Urban Development (HUD).

- **Seek Legal Advice:** Consult with a lawyer specializing in disability rights to ensure your case is well-documented and your complaint is thorough.

- **Contact Advocacy Groups:** Reach out to organizations like Disability Rights Advocates or the National Disability Rights Network for guidance and support.

- **Build a Support System:** Share your concerns with trusted friends or family members. Emotional support is invaluable when dealing with retaliation.

Building confidence as an advocate is a journey of growth, resilience, and empowerment. By equipping yourself with knowledge, developing effective communication skills, and fostering self-care, you can navigate challenges and assert your rights with poise. Remember, every act of advocacy contributes to a more inclusive and equitable society—not only for yourself but for others who face similar barriers.

Chapter 10: Connecting with Support Networks

Advocacy can feel like a daunting journey, but you don't have to walk it alone. Building strong support networks—whether through formal organizations, local resources, or personal connections—can bolster your efforts, provide essential guidance, and remind you that you are part of a broader community working toward equality and inclusion. This chapter delves into the importance of connecting with national and local disability rights organizations, cultivating personal relationships, and fostering a network of allies to amplify your advocacy efforts.

Advocacy Groups and Communities

Engaging with advocacy groups and disability rights organizations is a powerful way to amplify your voice and access essential resources. These organizations provide knowledge, training, legal aid, and platforms for collective action, ensuring that you are supported in your advocacy journey.

National Organizations

National disability advocacy organizations focus on systemic change and policy advocacy while also offering support to individuals. These groups often provide educational materials, legal guidance, and opportunities for community engagement.

- **Americans with Disabilities Act (ADA) National Network:** Offers comprehensive training and guidance on the ADA to individuals, businesses, and organizations. It's an excellent resource for understanding how the law protects your rights.

- **Disability Rights Advocates (DRA):** Specializes in high-impact litigation to fight for the rights of people with disabilities in areas such as education, healthcare, and public access.

- **National Disability Rights Network (NDRN):** A nationwide nonprofit supporting Protection and Advocacy (P&A) systems, which provide free legal services to individuals facing disability-related discrimination.

- **The Arc:** Focuses on promoting and protecting the rights of people with intellectual and developmental disabilities, offering resources for navigating education, employment, and housing challenges.

- **American Association of People with Disabilities (AAPD):** Works to advance the economic and political empowerment of people with disabilities, fostering leadership and civic engagement opportunities.

How National Organizations Can Help:

- **Educational Resources:** Access webinars, guides, and publications tailored to disability rights.

- **Policy Advocacy:** Participate in campaigns that influence legislation and public policy.

- **Legal Support:** Find attorneys or advocates to assist with discrimination claims or rights violations.

- **Community Engagement:** Join national events, such as Disability Pride Month activities or advocacy conferences, to connect with other advocates.

Local Resources

While national organizations provide a broad framework for advocacy, local groups address the unique needs of your community. Local resources are often more personalized and responsive to the specific challenges of your area.

- **Independent Living Centers (ILCs):** Provide direct services such as skills training, peer counseling, and help with accessing benefits or making homes more accessible.

- **Community Disability Organizations:** Many towns and cities have grassroots disability advocacy groups focused on issues like local transit accessibility or school inclusion.

- **Faith-Based and Cultural Groups:** Some churches, temples, or community centers offer disability-related programs tailored to specific cultural or religious communities.
- **Local Advocacy Coalitions:** Many communities have coalitions that work on specific issues, such as accessible voting, inclusive education, or affordable housing.

How to Connect Locally:

- **Online Directories:** Use resources like 211.org or Disability.gov to locate services in your area.
- **Community Events:** Attend meetings, workshops, or town halls hosted by local organizations.
- **Social Media Groups:** Search for local advocacy groups on platforms like Facebook or Meetup to connect with others who share your goals.
- **Networking:** Reach out to friends, family, or coworkers who might have connections to local resources.

Building a Personal Support System

While formal organizations provide crucial resources, a personal support system is equally important for maintaining emotional resilience and gaining practical assistance.

Mentorship

A mentor in the disability advocacy community can guide you through the complexities of your journey. Mentors can be experienced advocates, professionals in disability rights law, or even peers who have navigated similar challenges.

- **Benefits of Mentorship:**
    - Guidance on tackling legal or advocacy obstacles.
    - Emotional support and encouragement during difficult times.

- Insights into effective strategies for self-advocacy.

- **Finding Mentors:**
    - Look for mentorship programs through organizations like The Arc, NDRN, or local ILCs.
    - Attend advocacy events and build connections with experienced activists or professionals.
    - Seek mentors in your professional field who also share your experiences with disability.

Allies

Building a network of allies is critical for amplifying your voice and expanding the reach of your advocacy. Allies can include friends, family, colleagues, or community members who support your cause and can contribute to your efforts.

- **How Allies Can Help:**
    - Assist with logistical tasks, such as coordinating events or spreading awareness on social media.
    - Act as witnesses or advocates during interactions with employers, landlords, or service providers.
    - Provide emotional support when challenges arise.

- **Cultivating Allies:**
    - Educate potential allies about disability rights and the barriers you face.
    - Encourage them to participate in advocacy events or join campaigns.
    - Create opportunities for them to learn, such as sharing articles or inviting them to training sessions.

Tips for Building and Maintaining Support Networks

Creating and sustaining meaningful relationships within your advocacy network requires effort and intentionality. Here are some strategies for success:

- **Communicate Clearly:** Be open about your goals, challenges, and how others can help. Clear communication fosters trust and collaboration.

- **Be Inclusive:** Ensure your network reflects diverse perspectives, including individuals from different backgrounds, industries, and levels of experience.

- **Offer Mutual Support:** Advocacy is a two-way street. Offer your own time, knowledge, or resources to others in your network.

- **Celebrate Wins:** Take time to acknowledge and celebrate shared accomplishments, whether big or small. Recognition builds morale and reinforces commitment to the cause.

- **Stay Organized:** Use tools like calendars, group chats, or project management software to keep your network connected and aligned on shared goals.

Connecting with support networks—both formal and informal—empowers you to become a stronger advocate while fostering a sense of belonging and community. By engaging with national and local organizations, finding mentors, and recruiting allies, you can amplify your impact and sustain your efforts for systemic change. Together, these relationships create a foundation for personal growth, collective action, and meaningful progress toward a more inclusive society.

Chapter 11: Practical Tools for Navigating Daily Life

Where to File a Disability-Related Complaint

Here's a comprehensive list of agencies and organizations where individuals can file disability-related complaints, depending on the context of the issue:

Employment Complaints

1. **Equal Employment Opportunity Commission (EEOC)**

    o For complaints of workplace discrimination under the *Americans with Disabilities Act (ADA)* or *Rehabilitation Act*.

    o Website: www.eeoc.gov

    o Note: Complaints must be filed within 180 days of the discriminatory act (or 300 days in states with local fair employment practices agencies).

2. **State or Local Fair Employment Practices Agencies (FEPAs)**

    o Handles employment discrimination complaints at the state or local level, often overlapping with the EEOC.

    o Contact your state or local human rights commission.

Education Complaints

3. **U.S. Department of Education, Office for Civil Rights (OCR)**

    o For complaints against schools, colleges, or universities under *Section 504 of the Rehabilitation Act* or the *Individuals with Disabilities Education Act (IDEA)*.

    o Website: www.ed.gov/ocr

    o Note: Complaints must be filed within 180 days of the alleged discrimination.

4. **State Department of Education or Local School District**
    - For disputes about Individualized Education Plans (IEPs) or accommodations under IDEA.

Housing Complaints

5. **U.S. Department of Housing and Urban Development (HUD)**
    - For complaints related to housing discrimination under the *Fair Housing Act (FHA)*.
    - Website: www.hud.gov
    - Note: Complaints must be filed within one year of the alleged discrimination.

6. **State or Local Fair Housing Agencies**
    - Many states have their own agencies that enforce housing laws alongside HUD.

Public Accommodations Complaints

7. **U.S. Department of Justice (DOJ), Civil Rights Division**
    - For discrimination by businesses, public accommodations, or state/local government entities under ADA Title II or Title III.
    - Website: www.ada.gov
    - File complaints directly via email or mail through the DOJ's ADA Information Line.

Transportation Complaints

8. **U.S. Department of Transportation (DOT), Office of Aviation Consumer Protection**

- For air travel complaints under the *Air Carrier Access Act (ACAA)*.
- Website: www.transportation.gov/airconsumer

9. **Federal Transit Administration (FTA), Office of Civil Rights**
    - For complaints regarding accessibility of public transportation under ADA Title II.
    - Website: www.transit.dot.gov

Healthcare Complaints

10. **U.S. Department of Health and Human Services (HHS), Office for Civil Rights (OCR)**
    - For discrimination by healthcare providers or insurers under *Section 504 of the Rehabilitation Act* or the *Affordable Care Act*.
    - Website: www.hhs.gov/ocr
    - Note: Complaints must be filed within 180 days of the discriminatory act.

Social Security Disability Complaints

11. **Social Security Administration (SSA), Office of the Inspector General (OIG)**
    - For complaints about improper handling of disability benefits or accessibility at SSA offices.
    - Website: www.ssa.gov

Veterans Disability Complaints

12. **U.S. Department of Veterans Affairs (VA), Office of Resolution Management, Diversity, and Inclusion (ORMDI)**
    - For disability discrimination within VA services or benefits.

- o Website: www.va.gov

Telecommunications Complaints

13. Federal Communications Commission (FCC)

- o For complaints about telecommunications access (e.g., closed captioning, relay services) under the ADA.
- o Website: www.fcc.gov

Other Complaints

14. State Protection and Advocacy (P&A) Systems

- o Federally funded organizations providing legal advocacy for people with disabilities.
- o Find your state's P&A at www.ndrn.org.

15. Local Human Rights or Civil Rights Commissions

- o Many cities or counties have offices that address local disability discrimination issues.

16. Job Accommodation Network (JAN)

- o While not a complaint-filing agency, JAN provides expert guidance on workplace accommodations and resolving disputes.
- o Website: www.askjan.org

17. Nonprofits and Advocacy Groups

- o Groups like the *National Disability Rights Network (NDRN)* and *Disability Rights Education & Defense Fund (DREDF)* can provide support and resources.

Tips for Filing Complaints

- **Document Everything**: Keep detailed records of incidents, including dates, times, witnesses, and correspondence.

- **Deadlines**: Be mindful of filing deadlines, which vary by agency.

- **Legal Assistance**: Consider consulting a disability rights attorney for guidance.

Whether you're requesting accommodations, addressing discrimination, or preparing for important interactions, having a toolkit of practical resources can empower you to act confidently and effectively. This chapter provides detailed templates, comprehensive checklists, and curated resources to guide you through everyday advocacy and decision-making.

Sample Templates

Templates can save time and ensure your communication is clear and professional. The following templates are examples of letters and forms tailored to common scenarios, including requesting accommodations and filing complaints.

Sample Letter for Requesting Workplace Accommodations

[Your Name]
[Your Address]
[City, State, ZIP Code]
[Date]

[Employer's Name]
[Company Name]
[Address]
[City, State, ZIP Code]

Subject: Request for Reasonable Accommodation

Dear [Employer's Name],

I am writing to formally request a reasonable accommodation under the Americans with Disabilities Act (ADA). I have [specific condition or disability], which impacts my ability to [specific limitation]. To ensure I can perform the essential functions of my job effectively, I request the following accommodation(s):

- [Example: Adjustable desk to accommodate mobility needs.]
- [Example: Flexible work hours for medical appointments.]

Attached, you will find documentation from my healthcare provider supporting my request. I am happy to discuss these needs further to identify the best solutions.

Thank you for considering my request. Please let me know if additional information is needed, and I look forward to your response.

Sincerely,

[Your Name]

Sample Letter for Requesting Housing Accommodations

[Your Name]
[Your Address]
[City, State, ZIP Code]
[Date]

[Landlord's Name]
[Property Management Company]
[Address]
[City, State, ZIP Code]

Subject: Request for Reasonable Accommodation

Dear [Landlord's Name],

I am writing to request a reasonable accommodation under the Fair Housing Act. Due to my disability, I require [specific accommodation, e.g., installation of a wheelchair ramp, permission for an assistance animal, or a reserved parking space near the entrance].

This accommodation is necessary to ensure I can access and enjoy my housing. Attached is a letter from my healthcare provider confirming my need for this adjustment.

Please contact me if additional information is required. I appreciate your attention to this matter and look forward to a timely response.

Sincerely,

[Your Name]

Sample Complaint Letter for Disability Discrimination

[Your Name]
[Your Address]
[City, State, ZIP Code]
[Date]

[Recipient's Name]
[Organization Name]
[Address]
[City, State, ZIP Code]

Subject: Formal Complaint of Disability Discrimination

Dear [Recipient's Name],

I am filing this formal complaint to address an incident of disability discrimination that occurred on [specific date]. The incident took place at [specific location or organization].

As an individual with a disability, I experienced [specific discriminatory action, e.g., denial of reasonable accommodation, unequal treatment, or harassment]. Below are the details of the incident:

- **Date and Time:** [Include specifics.]
- **Description of Incident:** [Provide a clear and concise account of what happened.]
- **Individuals Involved:** [List the names and roles of those involved, if known.]

I believe these actions violate [specific law, such as the ADA, Fair Housing Act, or Air Carrier Access Act]. I respectfully request that this matter be investigated and appropriate corrective measures be taken.

I am available to provide additional information if needed. Thank you for your attention to this important matter.

Sincerely,
[Your Name]

Checklists and Action Plans

Having a structured plan can make challenging situations easier to navigate. Use the following checklists and action plans to stay organized and confident.

Preparing for Meetings

Meeting with an Employer

- Bring a copy of your job description.
- Prepare documentation of your disability, if necessary.
- List specific accommodations you're requesting.
- Obtain a letter from your healthcare provider, if applicable.
- Review the company's accommodation policy (if available).
- Bring a notepad, pen, or digital device to take notes.

Meeting with a Healthcare Provider

- Write a list of symptoms, concerns, or questions.
- Note any medications you are currently taking.
- Bring medical history or prior treatment records.
- Have insurance details and identification on hand.
- Include a support person if desired for clarity and advocacy.

Meeting with a Service Provider or Landlord

- Prepare a description of your accommodation needs.
- Bring relevant documentation, such as a doctor's letter.
- Note prior barriers or issues you've encountered.
- Have contact information for an advocate or legal representative, if applicable.

Steps to Take When Discrimination Occurs

1. **Document the Incident**

    o   Write down the date, time, and location.

    o   Record what happened, who was involved, and any witnesses.

    o   Keep copies of correspondence, emails, and written records.

2. **Gather Evidence**

    o   Take photos or videos of inaccessible spaces (if legally permissible).

    o   Collect statements from witnesses, if applicable.

3. **Report the Issue**

    o   File a complaint with the appropriate authority (e.g., employer, government agency, or transportation provider).

    o   Use one of the provided templates to draft your complaint.

4. **Seek Advocacy Support**

    o   Reach out to organizations or attorneys specializing in disability rights for advice and representation.

5. **Follow Up**

    o   Monitor the progress of your complaint.

    o   Document any retaliation or continued discrimination.

Helpful Resources

Hotlines and Legal Support

- **ADA Information Line:**
Phone: 1-800-514-0301 (voice) or 1-800-514-0383 (TTY).

- **Fair Housing Assistance Program (HUD)**:
  Phone: 1-800-669-9777.

- **Air Carrier Access Act Hotline**:
  Phone: 1-800-778-4838 (for airline complaints).

Advocacy Organizations

- **National Council on Independent Living (NCIL)**: Offers advocacy and support resources for independent living.

- **Job Accommodation Network (JAN)**: Provides guidance on workplace accommodations and disability employment issues.

- **Disability Rights Education and Defense Fund (DREDF)**: Focuses on legal advocacy and public policy.

Online Resources

- **ADA.gov**: Comprehensive guide to the ADA and enforcement.

- **Disability.gov**: Resources for housing, employment, healthcare, and more.

- **State Protection and Advocacy (P&A) Systems**: Local organizations that assist with disability-related legal issues.

By leveraging these practical tools, templates, and resources, you can navigate daily life with confidence, knowing that you are equipped to advocate effectively for your rights.

Appendices

The appendices provide an essential toolkit to deepen your understanding of disability rights and to equip you with practical resources for advocacy. Whether you're seeking detailed legal references, definitions of key terms, or connections to supportive networks, these sections offer comprehensive information to guide you on your journey.

Appendix A: Key Laws and Legal References for Further Reading

Understanding the laws that protect your rights as a person with a disability is foundational to effective advocacy. Below are summaries of the key laws, their applications, and where you can find more detailed information:

Americans with Disabilities Act (ADA)

- **Overview**: The ADA prohibits discrimination based on disability in various areas, including employment, public services, public accommodations, and telecommunications. It guarantees equal opportunities and reasonable accommodations for individuals with disabilities.

- **Key Provisions**:
    - Title I: Employment protections.
    - Title II: Access to public services and programs.
    - Title III: Accessibility in public accommodations and commercial facilities.
    - Title IV: Telecommunications services for individuals with hearing or speech disabilities.

- **Where to Learn More**: Visit the ADA's official website at ADA.gov.

Rehabilitation Act of 1973

- **Section 504**: Ensures that individuals with disabilities are not excluded from or denied benefits of federally funded programs.

- **Section 508**: Mandates accessible electronic and information technology for federal agencies.
- **Significance**: This law laid the groundwork for broader protections under the ADA.
- **Where to Learn More**: Explore resources at Section 508.gov.

Fair Housing Act (FHA)

- **Overview**: Protects individuals from discrimination in housing-related activities, such as renting, buying, and securing loans. It requires landlords and housing providers to accommodate people with disabilities.
- **Accommodations**: Examples include allowing service animals in pet-restricted housing and permitting reasonable structural modifications like wheelchair ramps.
- **Where to Learn More**: Visit the U.S. Department of Housing and Urban Development (HUD) at HUD.gov.

Air Carrier Access Act (ACAA)

- **Overview**: Governs the rights of people with disabilities in air travel, including boarding assistance, seating accommodations, and access to service animals.
- **Key Points**:
    - Airlines must provide disability-related assistance during the boarding, flight, and deplaning processes.
    - Airlines cannot charge fees for accommodations like mobility aids.
- **Where to Learn More**: Learn more through the Department of Transportation at DOT.gov.

Individuals with Disabilities Education Act (IDEA)

- **Overview**: Guarantees free and appropriate public education (FAPE) for children with disabilities. IDEA mandates individualized education programs (IEPs) and related services to support students in reaching their full potential.
- **Where to Learn More**: Visit the official IDEA site at IDEA.ed.gov.

Other Relevant Laws

- **Family and Medical Leave Act (FMLA):** Provides job-protected leave for medical or caregiving needs, including those related to disabilities.

- **Civil Rights of Institutionalized Persons Act (CRIPA):** Protects the rights of people in institutions, such as nursing homes and correctional facilities.

- **Equal Employment Opportunity Commission (EEOC):** Offers guidelines and enforcement for workplace protections under the ADA.

Appendix B: Glossary of Terms and Acronyms

This glossary helps clarify commonly used terms and acronyms in disability advocacy. Understanding these will empower you to navigate conversations, legal documents, and advocacy efforts more effectively.

Key Terms

- **Accommodation:** Adjustments or modifications that allow individuals with disabilities to fully participate in activities, services, or employment.

- **Accessibility:** The design of products, services, or environments to ensure they are usable by everyone, including individuals with disabilities.

- **Assistive Technology (AT):** Tools or devices that help individuals with disabilities perform tasks they might otherwise find difficult or impossible. Examples include screen readers, wheelchairs, hearing aids, and communication boards.

- **Barrier-Free Design:** An architectural and design approach that removes physical barriers, allowing full accessibility for individuals with disabilities.

- **Disability:** A physical or mental condition that substantially limits one or more major life activities, such as walking, seeing, hearing, or learning.

- **Disparate Impact:** A legal term referring to policies or practices that appear neutral but disproportionately affect individuals with disabilities or other protected groups.

- **Equal Access**: The principle that individuals with disabilities should have the same opportunities to participate in activities, use services, and access resources as everyone else, without additional barriers.

- **Essential Functions**: The fundamental duties of a job or role that an individual must be able to perform, with or without reasonable accommodation.

- **Inclusive Design**: Similar to universal design, this approach focuses on creating products, services, or environments that accommodate the widest range of users, including those with disabilities.

- **Program Accessibility**: A requirement under the ADA and Rehabilitation Act that ensures public entities make their programs and services accessible to individuals with disabilities.

- **Reasonable Accommodation**: Changes that enable individuals with disabilities to perform essential job functions or access services without undue burden on the provider.

- **Reasonable Modification**: Changes to policies, practices, or procedures to allow individuals with disabilities equal access to public spaces and services.

- **Service Animal**: A dog (or, in some cases, a miniature horse) specifically trained to perform tasks directly related to an individual's disability, such as guiding a person who is blind or alerting a person with epilepsy to an impending seizure.

- **Undue Hardship**: A legal concept under the ADA describing a significant difficulty or expense incurred by an employer or service provider when accommodating an individual with a disability.

- **Universal Design**: The creation of environments, products, and systems that are inherently accessible to all individuals, regardless of ability.

- **Web Accessibility**: The practice of designing websites and digital tools so they can be used effectively by people with disabilities, such as those who rely on screen readers or keyboard navigation.

Acronyms

- **ABA**: *Architectural Barriers Act* – A law requiring that federally funded buildings and facilities be accessible to individuals with disabilities.

- **ADA**: *Americans with Disabilities Act* – Landmark legislation that prohibits discrimination based on disability in employment, public services, public accommodations, and telecommunications.

- **ADAAG**: *ADA Accessibility Guidelines* – Technical standards that guide the design of facilities to ensure accessibility for individuals with disabilities under the ADA.

- **ACAA**: *Air Carrier Access Act* – Protects the rights of individuals with disabilities in air travel.

- **CAP**: *Computer/Electronic Accommodations Program* – A program offering assistive technology and services to federal employees and military personnel with disabilities.

- **EEOC**: *Equal Employment Opportunity Commission* – The federal agency that enforces laws against workplace discrimination.

- **FHA**: *Fair Housing Act* – Prohibits discrimination in the sale, rental, and financing of housing based on disability and other protected classes.

- **HUD**: *U.S. Department of Housing and Urban Development* – Enforces fair housing laws and ensures equal access to housing.

- **ICF**: *International Classification of Functioning, Disability, and Health* – A framework by the World Health Organization for describing and measuring health and disability at individual and population levels.

- **IDEA**: *Individuals with Disabilities Education Act* – Ensures students with disabilities receive free appropriate public education tailored to their individual needs.

- **JAN**: *Job Accommodation Network* – Provides free resources and guidance on workplace accommodations.

- **LEP**: *Limited English Proficiency* – While not exclusively disability-related, this designation often intersects with accessibility services, ensuring communication access for individuals with disabilities who are non-native English speakers.

- **OCR**: *Office for Civil Rights* – A division of the U.S. Department of Education responsible for enforcing federal civil rights laws in education, including disability-related protections.

- **P&A**: *Protection and Advocacy Systems* – Federally funded programs that advocate for the rights of individuals with disabilities.

- **RTAA**: *Rehabilitation Technology Assistance Act* – State-level programs that provide individuals with disabilities access to assistive technologies.

- **Section 504**: Part of the *Rehabilitation Act of 1973* prohibiting discrimination based on disability in any program or activity receiving federal financial assistance.

- **SSA**: *Social Security Administration* – Administers disability benefits programs like Supplemental Security Income (SSI) and Social Security Disability Insurance (SSDI).

- **Title II**: The part of the ADA that covers programs, activities, and services of public entities, ensuring equal access to government services.

- **Title III**: The part of the ADA that mandates equal access to public accommodations, such as restaurants, hotels, and theaters.

- **WAI**: *Web Accessibility Initiative* – A program under the World Wide Web Consortium (W3C) focused on improving web accessibility for individuals with disabilities.

Appendix C: Online and Local Resources

Access to resources can make a significant difference when advocating for your rights or seeking assistance. Below is a list of national, online, and local resources:

National Organizations

- **Disability Rights Education and Defense Fund (DREDF)**: Provides legal advocacy and training on disability rights. Website: DREDF.org
- **National Council on Independent Living (NCIL)**: Focuses on advancing independent living for people with disabilities. Website: NCIL.org
- **Job Accommodation Network (JAN)**: Offers guidance on workplace accommodations and the ADA. Website: AskJAN.org

Government Resources

- **ADA Information Line**: For questions about ADA rights, call 1-800-514-0301 (voice) or 1-800-514-0383 (TTY).
- **HUD Fair Housing Complaint Line**: Report housing discrimination at 1-800-669-9777.
- **Transportation Hotline**: File complaints regarding air travel at 1-800-778-4838.

Local Resources

- **Protection and Advocacy Systems (P&A)**: Every state has a P&A organization to provide legal and advocacy services. Find your state's agency at NDRN.org.
- **Centers for Independent Living (CILs)**: Local nonprofits that provide services to support independent living. Search for centers near you through NCIL's directory.

Support Hotlines

- **Crisis Text Line**: Text HOME to 741741 for free mental health support.
- **Legal Aid Services**: Many states offer legal aid for low-income individuals facing discrimination.

By leveraging these resources, laws, and tools, you can become a more confident and informed advocate, equipped to navigate the complexities of disability rights and achieve meaningful outcomes.

Dear Reader,

Thank you for taking the time to explore this book. My hope is that it has provided you with knowledge, tools, and confidence to navigate your rights as a person with a disability in all areas of daily life. Whether you're advocating for accommodations at work, fighting for access to housing, ensuring inclusivity in education, or addressing transportation barriers, this book is meant to empower you to stand firm in your rights and find support when you need it.

Disability advocacy is not just about knowing the law—it's about recognizing your worth, asserting your needs, and building a life that honors your unique abilities and aspirations. The path to inclusivity is not always easy, but by understanding your rights and connecting with supportive communities, you can create meaningful change in your own life and inspire systemic improvements that benefit everyone.

I hope this book serves as a valuable resource, whether you're facing a specific challenge or simply want to be better prepared for the future. If you feel overwhelmed at times, remember that advocacy is a journey, not a destination. Celebrate your wins, no matter how small, and know that every step forward makes a difference.

You are not alone in this journey. Countless individuals and organizations are working tirelessly to promote disability rights and inclusivity. By joining these efforts, whether through self-advocacy or collaboration with others, you contribute to a larger movement that is reshaping the world for the better.

You deserve a life of dignity, opportunity, and fulfillment—and you have the power to make that a reality.

With gratitude and encouragement,

Jana Lomax, J.D.

About the Author

Meet Jana Lomax, a tireless civil rights lawyer and investigator (and mom) on a mission to champion social justice and advocacy. Hailing from Kansas City, Missouri, Jana has carved out an impressive career working with various state and city civil rights agencies, where she has spearheaded hundreds of investigations into employment and public accommodations discrimination. Her extensive experience equips her with keen insights into the fight against discrimination and the pursuit of equity.

Jana brings a powerful and unique perspective to her legal work; she's Black, she's a woman, and she's the mother of child with Autism. She is deeply committed to amplifying marginalized voices and dismantling systemic barriers. Her personal journey fuels her advocacy for inclusive policies that empower individuals to recognize their rights and seek justice.

Jana's expertise encompasses a wide array of civil rights issues, and she is passionate about educating others on the critical importance of acknowledging and addressing discrimination. Through her writing and public service, she strives to inspire change and create a more equitable society for all.

When she's not advocating for justice, Jana enjoys cozy nights at home, indulging her inner foodie, diving into fantasy and thrillers—both in books and on screen—and cherishing time spent with family and friends in Kansas City, where she lives with her son.

www.ingramcontent.com/pod-product-compliance
Lightning Source LLC
Chambersburg PA
CBHW062322220526
45469CB00008B/2593